Analysing American Advice Books for Single Mothers Raising Sons

Analysing American Advice Books for Single Mothers Raising Sons

Essentialism, Culture and Guilt

Berit Åström

ANTHEM PRESS

Anthem Press
An imprint of Wimbledon Publishing Company
www.anthempress.com

This edition first published in UK and USA 2025
by ANTHEM PRESS
75–76 Blackfriars Road, London SE1 8HA, UK
or PO Box 9779, London SW19 7ZG, UK
and
244 Madison Ave #116, New York, NY 10016, USA

First published in the UK and USA by Anthem Press in 2023

© 2025 Berit Åström

The author asserts the moral right to be identified as the author of this work.

All rights reserved. Without limiting the rights under copyright reserved above, no part of this publication may be reproduced, stored or introduced into a retrieval system, or transmitted, in any form or by any means (electronic, mechanical, photocopying, recording or otherwise), without the prior written permission of both the copyright owner and the above publisher of this book.

British Library Cataloguing-in-Publication Data
A catalogue record for this book is available from the British Library.

Library of Congress Control Number: 2024951003
A catalog record for this book has been requested.

ISBN-13: 978-1-83999-477-7 (Pbk)
ISBN-10: 1-83999-477-0 (Pbk)

This title is also available as an e-book.

CONTENTS

1. Introduction: Childcare and Advice in Times of Change — 1
2. Gender: Borderwork, Science and the Dangerous Mother — 15
3. Class and Race: Expectations of Mothers and Sons — 37
4. Reinstating the Father: Fathers in Advice Books for Mothers — 65
5. Conclusion — 77

Appendix — 79
Notes — 83
Bibliography — 87
Index — 99

Chapter 1

INTRODUCTION: CHILDCARE AND ADVICE IN TIMES OF CHANGE

The single mother is a divisive figure in US society that has incurred great ire from various voices in society, such as in the media and politics. She is often constructed as a moral hazard or a financial drain on society. A particular target in public conversations is the single mother raising a son, who is also represented as a threat to the child.[1] Freelance author Shawn James, for example, sums up this attitude in his blog post, 'Ways Single Mothers Destroy Their Sons', in which he writes that '[t]he most toxic environment for a boy growing up is in a single mother household' (James 2013, 43). James' claim clearly resonates with the public and has been referenced by many bloggers and YouTubers since.[2] The single mother is often portrayed as a 'deviant' (De Benedictis 2012, 3). Through her deficient mothering, she is 'responsible for societal collapse through male juvenile delinquency' as sociologist Sara De Benedictis notes in an analysis of neoliberal discourse on single mothers (2012, 3). Faced with such unrelenting criticism, the single mother may turn to advice books for help.

In this she would not be alone. Up to one-half of Americans are said to have bought a self-help book at some point in their life (McGee 2005, 11), making them a 'visible and powerful force in American society' (Starker 2008, 1). As sociologist Micki McGee observes, advice books 'are available to cover any and all issues, with titles specialized to address every market segment' (2005, 12). One very popular market segment is parenting books. Amazon, for example, lists over 70 000 titles in this category, which places it on a par with genres such as career books (over 60 000 books) and dieting books (over 60 000 books).[3] Such numbers suggest that many parents turn to parenting books for advice. Whether they take that advice is another matter. The books cannot tell us what parents actually *do*, but ethnographers and historians have tended to use 'parent advice literature ... as a window on cultural norms for childrearing' (Hoffman 2009, 16). The books can tell us what ideas of parents, parenting and children are circulating in society, and accepted as reasonable (Faircloth, Hoffman, and Layne 2013, 9). The books also tell us what childrearing practices are regarded as problematic and how 'parents', in particular singular mothers, are 'produced through discourses of what they are not, of what they (seem to) fail to do' (2013, 9).[4]

Advice books,[5] by their very nature, must take as their starting point that the reader is deficient in some way; otherwise, she would not need the book in the first place. Sandra Dolby, in her study of the genre, refers to the structure of 'lack and lack liquidated' (2005). The advice books aimed at the single mother show her what she is lacking and then instruct her on how to change her ways, making the books 'mother-rearing tracts' to borrow a term from Nancy Pottisham Weiss' analysis of the maternal education movement in the United States (1978, 31).[6] In this study, I analyse the way a broad selection of advice books construct mothers and sons, as well as what they reveal about contemporary cultural norms for childrearing in the United States, attitudes towards the roles and functions of mothers and fathers in the family, the construction of masculinity and, by extension, how society is expected to function. One of the most striking assumptions that emerge from the areas discussed and the language employed in the books is that single mothers cannot successfully raise sons to men. Whilst claiming to offer comfort and support, a large proportion of the books level criticism towards the mothers: for being single, for keeping fathers away from their sons, for endangering their sons' physical and mental health and for making it impossible for them to form healthy adult relationships with women and other men.

This study connects with and builds on previous studies of books about raising boys, such as Michael Gurian's *The Wonder of Boys* (2006) and William Pollack's *Real Boys* (1998). Analysing these books, Kristin J. Anderson and Christina Accomando show how the authors perpetuate stereotypical and essentializing ideas of gender and parenting, in the process presenting boys as victims of an 'anti-boy culture' (2002). They point to the danger of these books: how they have influenced policy debates by 'produc[ing] an unsupported backlash against the brief gains in research on women and girls' (2002, 511). Sarah C. Hunter and Damien W. Riggs have further demonstrated how these books afford a very restricted range of identities for boys. What is seen as the '*normal*' boy has very narrow parameters, and anything outside that, for example, being homosexual, sensitive or uncertain, is not a 'valid subject position for a boy' (2015, 118–119, original emphasis). Looking at how these books address risks and responsibilities, Kristin J. Anderson, Jessica George and Jessica Nease discuss how the authors not only place greater demands on mothers than fathers but also how the mothers are constructed as constituting a risk to sons, 'represented as jealous, lacking boundaries, insecure, and in constant danger of veering into child abuse' (2002, 212). The essentialist approach to parenting, the restricted roles afforded to boys and the construction of the bad and dangerous mothers are also aspects evidenced in the material I analyse.

The aforementioned studies are of books on raising boys. Susan Sandretto and Karen Nairn have conducted a study of books specifically targeting mothers of sons, from the point of the supposed 'boy crisis in education' (2019, 328). They point to how the notion that '[m]mothers are bad for boys' is often reiterated and, when it is refuted, authors still draw on 'essentialising discourses about how mothers should parent their sons' (2019, 339). These notions and discourses are also present in my material.

The present study thus takes the studies referenced earlier as a starting point and develops my earlier pilot study, 'Advice Books for Single Mothers Raising Sons: Biology, Culture and Guilt' (2021). That study, like those outlined earlier, restricted itself to an analysis of gender, of how mothers, fathers and sons were constructed discursively in the material. In this book. I complement that analysis with investigations into class and race, reading the material through an intersectional lens. This approach shows the heterogeneity of the books, how the expected roles, attitudes and behaviours differ depending on the social and cultural context of authors and intended readership. For instance, although mother blame features in almost all the books, African American and White mothers are blamed for different actions and attitudes.

In the rest of this introduction, I will give a brief overview of how the structure and the idea of the American family have changed in recent decades, before moving on to a discussion of changes in attitudes towards children and childrearing. Following that, there is a short discussion of how the focus of advice books on childrearing has shifted before I introduce the corpus of advice books analysed. The chapter ends with an overview of the remaining chapters of the book.

American Families – Tradition and Change

Although societal structures can be said to be permanently in flux, the American family is perceived to have changed a great deal over recent decades. As Lynne Casper and Suzanne Bianchi note in their study of American families, the concept of family now may encompass several sets of parents (biological and adopted), some with new partners, step- and half-siblings, as well as three or more sets of grandparents (Casper and Bianchi 2002). There are also what Susan Golombok refers to as 'new families', which include 'lesbian mother families, gay father families, families headed by single-mothers by choice and families created by assisted reproductive technologies involving in vitro fertilization (IVF), egg donation, donor insemination, embryo donation and surrogacy' (2015, 3). The concept of family is widening beyond that of a heterosexual, married couple and their biological children. In fact, marriage is seemingly becoming less important in the definition of a family. Increasing numbers of people choose to cohabit rather than marry, and more people have children outside of marriage than 30 years ago (Marsh et al. 2007, 735). However, approximately half of the children born out of wedlock live with their fathers as well as their mothers (Golombok 2015, 2), which speaks against the stereotypical image that children born out of wedlock are the unplanned result of short-term relationships.

Added to these varieties of families are also those headed by single parents, particularly single mothers. According to data from the 2020 US Census, approximately 18.5 million children live in single-parent households and of those about 15.3 million live with their mothers (Hemez and Washington 2021). Single mothers are not a homogeneous category, however. Some live on their own, some cohabit with a new partner (who may not take any part in the raising of the children) and some live in the home of their own parents or other relatives. Their employment conditions vary as well, but overall US Census statistics paint the picture of poor women in difficult circumstances. However, single mothers by choice – those who have either adopted or chosen artificial reproductive technologies (ARTs) to conceive without a partner – tend to be better off, financially and socially, than other single mothers.

Just as single mothers are heterogeneous, so are the supposedly absent fathers of their children. The concept of 'father absence' or 'fatherlessness' has been discussed by, for example, David Blankenhorn (1996) and David Popenoe (1999) and presented as a great problem. Blankenhorn terms it 'our most urgent social problem' in the subtitle to his book *Fatherless America*. Yet, defining father absence is as complex as defining the single mother. In a study on fatherhood and masculinities, William Marsiglio and Joseph Pleck discuss the methodological problems with the concept, particularly when going beyond the simplistic idea of the father's absence from household (2005). The father may be a soldier deployed abroad for a time, or have the kind of job that takes him on the road two weeks out of three. The child may live with the father on weekends or during the summer holidays. Some children have fathers who live nearby, seeing the child on an almost daily basis. All these situations may be defined as father absence, but need not be. Nor does the absence of a father necessarily lead to negative outcomes for the child, as they point out; the 'context in which father absence occurs', for example, the mother's age, social network and financial situation may make a world of difference (2005, 253).

American family structures are thus quite diverse. But the family structures presented in the advice books analysed in this study do not acknowledge these diversities and complexities. Single-mother households are constructed as problematic because of the lack of a father. Lesbian partnerships are treated as single-mother households, since there is not a man present (e.g., Allen and Dickerson 2012, 99). Two-parent households with heterosexual married parents are referenced as the norm, the ultimate goal and the wished-for outcome, even by authors who are themselves single.

Changing Attitudes to Childrearing

The vulnerable child

Childrearing has always been a source of anxiety for parents, particularly in societies where child mortality was high (see, e.g., Cunningham 2005). Parents would try to find ways of ensuring that the children survived. This is reflected both in lay practices surrounding childbirth and childrearing and in advice given in conduct and advice books (see for instance Eccles 1982; Fildes 1986; Hardyment 2007). What is evident in the advice literature in England and the United States is the shift from physical concerns in the older literature to mental concerns in twentieth and twenty-first century texts.

Seventeenth- and eighteenth-century English texts, such as Jane Sharp's *The Midwives Book* (1671) and William Cadogan's *An Essay upon Nursing and the Management of Children from their Birth to Three Years of Age* (1757), warn mothers about the physical dangers that might threaten their children if they are fed the wrong things or their swaddling is not changed often enough (Åström 2015a). In the nineteenth century, there was a marked increase in the publication of childrearing manuals by doctors such as Andrew Combe, Pye Henry Chavasse and Thomas Bull, which were also popular in the United States (Hardyment 2007). These books also relied on what I have termed a 'narrative of fear', suggesting that the child lives in constant danger and that some of that danger emanates from the mother (Åström 2015b). However, the dangers were still imagined as predominantly physical.

As the nineteenth century changed into the twentieth, the medicalization of childcare in the United States increased, as Rima Apple (2006) and Peter Stearns (2003) have discussed, bringing new fears about children's development. Uncertainties brought on by economic and social changes as the century progressed, such as men's diminished breadwinner role and the rise in divorces, led parents to doubt themselves as adequate parents, redefine their children's roles and see them as more vulnerable (Stearns 2003). In his analysis of parental anxiety in the United States during the twentieth century, Stearns has pointed to the paradox that as children's lives became safer and better, parents came increasingly to view them as vulnerable, both physically and emotionally (2003). What was heralded as the century of the child 'became rather a century of anxiety about the child and about parents' own adequacy' (2003, 1). Over the century, a number of issues came and went as causes for concern, such as, poor posture, left-handedness or hyperactivity (2003, 1–2). In tandem with these concerns came the experts, telling parents, for example, that children must sleep in their own beds and must also sleep ten hours per night (2003, 47). A number of these issues were linked to maternal inadequacy, such as Donald Winnicott's claim that lack of maternal devotion could lead to autism and John Bowlby identifying physical separation from the mother as 'a pathogenic factor' (Davis 2012, 120, 122).

Childrearing thus became increasingly difficult, since it now also encompassed the children's intellectual stimulation and development, causing parents to worry more about the children's mental and emotional health, about '[e]motional and psychological risks' (Stearns 2003, 19). Frank Furedi, in his book *Paranoid Parenting*, notes how, at the turn of the twentieth century, young children are regarded as 'intensely vulnerable and highly impressionable', particularly to the effects of the parents (2008, 40). This vulnerability has been expressed in terms such as 'infant determinism' and 'parent causality' (Faircloth, Hoffman, and Layne 2013, 3). What happens, or does not happen, to the infant will affect the rest of its life, and it is always the parents' fault.

From childrearing to parenting

Increasingly, then, childrearing has come to be seen as something too difficult to be entrusted to parents. In their book *Parenting in Global Perspective*, Charlotte Faircloth, Diane M. Hoffman and Linda L. Layne make a distinction between *childrearing* and *parenting*. Childrearing is simply the 'care activities associated with traditional kinship roles' and thus, on the surface at least, something that anyone can do. Parenting, on the other hand, a term that came into widespread use in the 1950s, is defined as 'an activity that is increasingly taken to require a specific skill-set', something that requires knowledge of the latest research and ideally endorsed by experts (2013, 1). Parenting is something that must be taught and acquired; it is potentially problematic.

Jan Macvarish has studied how politics and science have become enmeshed, in what she calls 'neuroparenting' (2016). The intensive parenting of previous decades, manifested for example in the attachment theory and ideas of co-sleeping and exclusive breastfeeding, is now coupled with supposed scientific findings, bolstered with, for instance, MRI images, telling parents to worry about their child's brain development, since '"every day is a critical period"', (Macvarish 2016, 2). These ideas are put forward, not so much by scientists as by 'philanthropists, politicians, social activists and "moral entrepreneurs"' (2016, 10). They use the claims to explain away social problems caused by financial and social inequality. Poor parenting becomes the cause of 'politically graspable social problems such as a lack of educational attainment, low wages and ill health' (2016, 8). In this way, 'social problems such as inequality, poverty, educational underachievement, violence and mental illness are best addressed through "early intervention" programmes to protect or enhance emotional and cognitive aspects of children's brain development' (Macvarish, Lee, and Lowe 2014, 793). The problems caused by an unequal society thus become the responsibility of individual parents.

These ideas resonate with neoliberal attitudes towards parenting, where parents are made responsible not only for their children but also for 'the economy, the locality and the prosperity of society overall' (De Benedictis 2012, 2). This is particularly evident in relation to single mothers, who, De Benedictis argues, are expected to 'replace state support and build localities with an entrepreneurial spirit' through their own pluck and resourcefulness (2012, 3, 6). This will be further discussed in Chapter 3.

'Backlash books'

Many of the advice books analysed in my study take their inspiration and information from another genre of books, which appears to be occasioned by some of the social, economic and demographic changes that took place during the twentieth century, in particular the feminist movement.

Beginning in the 1990s, books began to be published which expressed a concern that boys were at a disadvantage in contemporary society. They articulated what sociologist Martin Mills, in his study of 'backlash blockbusters', has termed the '"what about the boys?" debate' (2003, 57). In this debate, it is claimed that too much time and resources are spent on helping girls, and boys are falling behind. One of the first books was Michael Gurian's *The Wonder of Boys: What Parents, Mentors, and Educators Can Do to Shape Boys into Exceptional Men*, first published in 1996 (2006). In the book, which he has followed up with a number with similar titles and in a similar vein, Gurian explains how boys work biologically and what they need socially in order to become men. In the preface to the tenth anniversary edition of *The Wonder of Boys*, he writes about the difficulties he had in getting the book published – it was rejected by 26 publishers, who only wanted books about girls. It was assumed that nobody wanted to read about the difficult problems that boys faced, nor did anyone want to read a book grounded in neurobiology, which claimed that boys' and girls' brains were substantially different. The preface articulates the two points that are central to the backlash books – boys suffer because girls are continually privileged, in school as well as socially, and boys and girls are so different that they might as well belong to different species. They require very different treatment when growing up, and a woman, who has no embodied experience of being a boy, is therefore unable to address the needs of a boy.

Gurian's book was followed by many similar ones, for example, Christina Hoff Sommers' *The War Against Boys: How Misguided Policies Are Harming Our Young Men* ([2000] 2013) and Leonard Sax's *Boys Adrift: The Five Factors Driving the Growing Epidemic of Unmotivated Boys and Underachieving Men* ([2007] 2016). One of the most recent books is William Farrell and John Gray's *The Boy Crisis* (2018).[7] Like most of the backlash books, Farrell sees the boy crisis as manifested in an 'increase in crime, incarceration, school shootings, domestic violence, rape, drugs, problems in mental health, physical health, poverty, unemployment, and [high] drop-out rates' (2018, 114). He points to two causes for this deplorable situation: the fact that boys are physically more vulnerable than girls and the great number of absent fathers, what he calls 'dad-deprivation' (2018, 105). This dad-deprivation is not only responsible for teenage boys committing suicide[8] but also higher taxes and increased ISIS recruitment (2018, 106, 114).

Writers such as Gurian and Farrell are noteworthy since they are very influential through their publications and public appearances and, in Gurian's case, the Gurian Institute, which aims to help parents, teachers, mental health professionals and community leaders, help boys and girls develop to the best of their ability through 'brain-based, research-driven' training (Gurian 2022). Both men illustrate Macvarish's observation that neuroparenting is generally not promoted by scientists. Gurian, who admits on his website that his 'career has not exactly followed the expected path of his completed degrees', has no education concerning boys' emotional, mental or physical development except for some course work in educational psychology in 2000 (2022). Farrell's qualifications are in Political Science. In their books, however, they give advice on, for example, child psychology and education. They also make references to scientific research in order to support their claims. The way Gurian and Sax use science has been referred to as 'shockingly careless, tendentious and even dishonest. Their over-interpretation and mis-interpretation of scientific research is so extreme that it becomes a form of fabrication' (qtd in Fine 2010, 165).[9] Their claims about boys' biology and the effects of dad-deprivation are then unquestioningly repeated by the authors of advice books.

Advice Books

Advice books specifically addressing childrearing draw on a very long history, although not in quite the same format as present-day books. In Europe, authors such as Erasmus of Rotterdam (1526), Elizabeth Clinton, Countess of Lincoln (1622), Dr William Cadogan (1757) and Dr Andrew Combe (1860) published works in which they explained how children should be treated. The focus of the advice in these books tended to be on breastfeeding, choice of wet nurses and a suitable diet mixed in with religious advice and advice to husbands and wives (Dod and Cleaver 1605). The first advice books in the US tended to be on the subject of how to live a devout life, such as Samuel Hardy's *Guide to Heaven* (1673) (Starker 2008, 14). Steven Starker, writing specifically on advice books in the United States, notes that the genre has since developed from 'a source of moral guidance' to functioning more as a source of 'useful and practical knowledge' (2008, 15). As Micki McGee notes in her critical study of self-help books, this type of literature 'defines its readers as insufficient' (McGee 2005, 18). Such an address 'may foster, rather than quell' the 'anxieties' of the readers (2005, 17). Sandra Dolby, although taking a more sanguine view of the genre, agrees that the advice books follow the structure of beginning with 'a suggestion that something is wrong with us' before giving 'a suggestion of what might be done to correct the problem' (2005, 4–5). Establishing the reader as lacking in knowledge or skills is particularly prevalent in contemporary advice books aimed at American parents. Although the specifics may vary, advice books on parenting generally cover the same ground: school, work (chores at home, summer jobs, volunteering), entertainment (screen time, sports, music lessons, the dangers of rap music) as well as health (mental and physical), sexuality (dating) and moral development.

The corpus

The titles analysed in this study were gathered from the websites of Amazon and Barnes and Noble. The books were selected primarily on content, on to what extent they actually give advice on how (single) mothers ought to raise their sons. This excludes, for example, Laveda M. Jones' '*Raising a Prince without a King*' (2015). Although advertising itself as answering the question 'How do you equip your son to become a successful man, when you have no male role model in his life?', the book is rather an autobiography detailing her emotional and spiritual recovery after her divorce; in fact, there is no advice given specifically on raising sons.

The books included in the study are thus aimed at mothers raising sons, and I have prioritized books that specifically target single mothers. However, in some cases, where relevant, I have included books that also address married mothers, such as Meg Meeker's *Strong Mothers, Strong Sons: Lessons Mothers Need to Raise Extraordinary Men* (2015). In such books, fathers tend to be left out, giving the impression that childrearing is only the mother's concern even in a two-parent, heterosexual household. I have also included a few books which primarily address the raising of boys, such as Steve Biddulph's *Raising Boys: Why Boys Are Different – and How to Help Them Become Happy and Well-Balanced Men* (2013), since they, in addition to generally addressing only mothers, also promote the idea that boys are so fundamentally different from girls that mothers run the risk of damaging their sons.

Since the aim of this study is to investigate how the advice books construct mothers and sons, I have paid less attention to publication figures and publishing houses. This is not a reception study, but a study into what norms and ideals are promoted and reproduced. It is of course noteworthy that major publishers such as Random House (through its imprints Tarcher Perigee and Ballantine Books) and Simon & Schuster (through its imprint Adams Media) regard it as financially viable to publish these books, but those books are no more interesting for this study than those published by smaller presses, such as Atlantic Publishing Group, or as a print on demand via Amazon's publishing platform CreateSpace.

The resulting corpus consists of 38 books published between 2001 and 2020. The authors are either White or African American – I have not been able to find any books written by, for example, Asian American or Latinx authors. Six of the books were written by two authors – one woman and one man. One book was written by two women. Of the rest, 16 were written by women and 15 by men. The authors come from diverse fields and backgrounds, ranging from medical doctors and clinical psychologists to social workers to lawyers, businessmen and youth ministers who were themselves raised by single mothers. There is very little difference in content or reader address between male or female authors, single or writing in pairs. There are, however, differences dependent on class or race, which will be discussed in Chapter 3. To make it easier to keep track of the authors, I have provided an appendix listing information given in the books or on the authors' websites, regarding their academic qualifications, professions, race and other pertinent information they choose to share.

All the authors establish their authority as experts on the rearing of sons, but through different strategies. As Dolby writes, a common feature of advice books is to place the author's academic or professional credentials on the cover (2005, 8). So do, for example, Meg Meeker, MD, and Dr Josef A. Passley. Some authors put their titles on the cover even when the degrees are not directly relevant, as does Dr William C. Small, who holds a PhD in Religious Studies. Other authors, however, make a virtue out of the fact that they are not academics but instead have real-life experience. Donna Joyce, for example, reiterates throughout her book that she shares the experiences of her readers – 'a single mom myself' – and promises that the advice in the book will be relevant to real lives and not 'mumbo-jumbo psychoanalytic nonsense' or 'psychobabble crap' that is of no practical help (2018, 2, 80). Similarly, John P. Dennis lists all the things he is not: 'I am not an academician, a scholar, a marriage & family therapist, a psychologist, or a specialist in the area of parental studies'. Instead, he is 'a concerned Dad … writing … from a male perspective' (2015, 13–14). These authors promise to help the reader through common sense and experience of what actually works. In short, the ways in which the authors have acquired their authority vary, but the end result is always that the authors have the experience and knowledge needed to advise single mothers on how best to raise their sons.

Advice books often re-package what is already known and present it as something new or present their advice as a new way of relating to whatever issue is addressed (Dolby 2005, 14). The authors in my corpus also do that in various ways. One way is to suggest that although many mothers and sons may suffer from not being able to communicate, this has not been generally recognized before, making the author feel 'compelled to write this book' (Meeker 2015, xv). Another approach is to present the issue of single mothers' inability to raise sons as so sensitive or problematic that it has until now only been 'whispered about' (Lewis 2010, 67), that it is 'one of the elephants in the room rarely addressed' (Dennis 2015, 10). The authors thus position themselves as experts and their texts as breaking new ground, helping single mothers with the problem of raising sons.

According to Dolby, advice books tend to present 'a critique of culture', to 'challenge some of its traditional beliefs' and suggest ways in which the culture may be changed (2005, 14). The advice books I study do offer up a critique, but they are motivated, not only by the discourse of the vulnerable child but also by recent changes to US family structures. In many cases, contemporary society is described as under threat from, for example, feminism and political correctness. Many of the authors present the reduction in marriages, increase in cohabitation, as well as the perceived increase[10] in the number of single-parent families as a problem, suggesting that traditional family values are under threat. There is a moralizing undertone to many of the books and several of the authors exhort the mother readers to fix a broken society through what sociologist Andrea Doucet refers to as three 'parental responsibilities' (2018, x). Adapting Sarah Ruddick's seminal re-conceptualization of mothering and maternal thinking to encompass parenting, Doucet defines these parental responsibilities as 'emotional, community/social and moral' (2018, x). These are the areas that the advice authors also focus on. Generally using a direct address of 'you', the mother reader is told to safeguard her son's emotional development (by toughening him up, or by being empathetic), to make sure that he becomes a productive member of society and takes his responsibility as a man and to vouchsafe his moral development. This is neatly summed up by Richard Bromfield and Cheryl Erwin, who promise to help the reader 'foster [in her son] healthy attitudes towards women and sex, promote educational and career success' as well as make the most of the influence of male role models (2001, xiv). The tone differs, however. Some authors, such as Meeker (2015) and Mardi Allen and James Dickerson (2012), use a relatively detached and clinical style with few personal comments or details. Others, such as Dennis (2015) and MaryAnne Howland (2020), use a much more personal and emotional style, with a focus on autobiography.

Starker notes that many advice books rely heavily on anecdotal evidence rather than information based on science, and they employ a prescriptive rather than descriptive approach (2008, 8–9). This is very noticeable in most of the books in my corpus. Health professionals and lay people alike use a number of anecdotes, stories about patients, celebrities such as Ringo Starr and Tom Cruise, or residents in their neighbourhood as not only illustrations of particular problems and solutions, but also as evidence. There are very few references to actual research, and when this is given, no sources are given beyond, possibly, a name. Usually, it is simply stated that research has shown, for example, that male infants are less aware of faces than female infants (Biddulph 2015, 14), or that a teenage boy's corpus callosum is 25 per cent smaller than a teenage girl's (Panettieri 2008, 19).

Part of establishing authority as an advice author, Jennifer Courtney writes in her analysis of domestic advice books for men, is to show 'good will (apparent concern for the good of the audience)' (2009, 70). This is attempted by some advice authors by praising the mother readers' importance to society, as 'the backbone of this nation' (Anderson 2017, x), 'the backbone of our society' (Joyce 2018, 119). Single mothers are 'walking superheroes' (Phillips 2018, 12) and the 'supreme nurturers of the universe' (Dennis 2015, 17). Almost all authors begin in this way, even though many of them will display a much more critical attitude later in the books, as will be discussed in Chapter 3.

As stated earlier, the single mother is a diverse character. Most of the advice books in this corpus acknowledge that there are different ways in which a woman might find herself single: through widowhood, divorce or never marrying. This acknowledgement is often prefaced with the phrase 'it doesn't matter how you came to be single' suggesting that to other people it might matter, that there is a potential for blame.[11] A few of the authors also note that there is the option of single adoption or ARTs. The single mothers by choice, SMCs, are rarely addressed, however. Nor are the widowed mothers, except for sections on how they should not let their grief affect the boy. The single mothers most often addressed are those separated from the fathers of their children, be it through a formal divorce or the end of a relationship.

Stressing that being a single parent is not inherently wrong, the authors still privilege 'family values', where a family should consist of 'a father-head earning an adequate family wage, a stay-at-home wife and mother, and children', which excludes many households, as Patricia Hill Collins notes (2009, 53). The authors tend to write from a position that children fare best if they grow up in a home with two married parents of the opposite sex. They also tend to assume tacitly that the readers are religious and active in some form of religious community. Some also explicitly argue for making sure that the sons take part in religious observances. Several of the authors explicitly express a desire for a return to a previous era, usually their own childhood, when relationships and childrearing were simpler. This might explain why there is little evidence of contemporary contexts, such as the economic downturn in 2008, or political developments.[12]

Overview of the Chapters

Chapter 2 analyses the corpus from the point of view of gender – how the books construct and represent motherhood, fatherhood and boyhood. The books rely heavily on essentialist views of sex and gender. Drawing on misrepresented scientific findings, a narrative is constructed in which mothers and sons cannot understand each other. The chapter also discusses the construction of masculinity, heteronormativity and the representation and understanding of sexuality in the books.

Chapter 3 analyses the books in terms of race and gender of authors and intended readership. A focus on gender alone may easily give the appearance of greater homogeneity amongst the books than there is, but this chapter shows that depending on race and class there are pronounced differences between what is expected of mothers and sons, of what can be achieved and how in terms of raising the boys, of what dangers and fears are anticipated for the boys and the way the mother reader is addressed.

Chapter 4 returns to the gender question, with a focus on fathers. It takes as its starting point the observation that although they are ostensibly absent in the narrative – these are, after all, books aimed at single mothers – the fathers are very much a presence. This chapter argues that the books are really more about men as fathers than about single mothers and their sons. Placing the books in the context of changing perceptions of fatherhood in the United States, I investigate the way in which some of the authors articulate a competition between mothers and fathers, attempting to establish the father as the more suitable parent.

I also analyse what might seem to be an unstated counternarrative. Reading between the lines, it may be possible to detect an understanding that children are better off without (biological) fathers. I further include a brief analysis of nine books aimed at single fathers raising daughters, particularly from the point of view of motivation for the books, reader address, expectations on the role of the father and paternal dating, which is treated very differently from maternal dating.

The conclusion draws all these strands together and raises some questions for the future. There seems to be no shortage of books giving advice to single mothers raising sons. As a genre, they tap into the centuries-old received wisdom that women, particularly mothers, are harmful to boys (see e.g. Plant 2010). The fact that it is now possible to self-publish quite easily via Amazon or other platforms seems to only increase the number of books. Even if one may assume that a great number of these books are only read by a few, the impulse to write them speaks to a perceived cultural need that is not met by the public conversations about families and parenting that are taking place currently.

Chapter 2

GENDER: BORDERWORK, SCIENCE AND THE DANGEROUS MOTHER

The explicit purpose of the advice books in this study is to help single mothers raise their sons. In doing so the authors outline a number of supposed problems, including how to teach and promote masculinity and how a boy can be made into a man without a man in the house. The stated intention of some of the authors is to rescue boys from a society that has turned its back on them and, in the process, get US society itself back on track. The unspoken assumption of a number of the authors is the conviction that humanity is dichotomous – that there is a basic, foundational difference between men and women. In this, the authors turn to scientific research that will support their claims that there are essential, biological differences between men and women, which will not only translate into differences in parenting carried out by mothers and fathers but also in insurmountable differences between mothers and sons.

The chapter begins with an overview of the concepts of sex and gender as they have been developed and applied by scientists as well as journalists and other lay people to support societal and cultural notions of masculinity and femininity. Then follows an overview of some of the central questions of masculinity studies, before moving on to an analysis of the advice books. The first section analyses the way the books construct and enforce perceived biological differences between men and women and, by extension, mothers and sons. Then follows an analysis of how the books construct masculinity, how this masculinity is intended to be taught to boys and what roles are afforded to the boys. The chapter concludes with an analysis of how heteronormativity is expressed in the books, both in terms of family structure and in assumptions of sexuality.

Sex and Gender

In 1972, sexologists John Money and Anke Erhardt published *Man & Woman, Boy & Girl*, in which they brought the view of sex and gender as 'separate categories' to a wider audience (Fausto-Sterling 2000, 3). In this view, sex pertains to body parts and reproduction, whereas gender is the 'internal conviction that one is either male or female (gender identity) and the behavioural expression of that conviction' (2000, 3). Developing this idea, post-structuralist feminists, such as Judith Butler, question the notion that gender is a 'stable identity' which governs one's actions (1999, 179). Butler instead sees gender as 'an identity tenuously constituted in time' through 'the *stylized repetition of acts*' – gender is regarded as performative (1999, 179, original italics). Gender is thus something one does, not something one is, and it is not determined by the reproductive organs one was born with. In fact, those organs themselves can add to the complexity, as biologist Anne Fausto-Sterling has shown. In her book *Sexing the Body* (2000), she discusses how sex, like gender, can be viewed as constructed. Fausto-Sterling reveals how cultural and societal concerns and pre-existing expectations cause scientists to reduce intersex individuals into either of two sexes, with strict demarcations. She gives as an example a child that is born with fully functional male and female sexual organs. It is assumed that the child must be made to conform to one of two categories, male or female, and a choice is made. This choice is then reinforced with surgery and hormone treatment. In this way 'sex is, literally, constructed' (2000, 27).

In the current debates of identity construction and transgender issues, as well as the legal, physical and emotional rights of transgender people, the lines between men, women and intersex people are increasingly blurred. The notion that an individual's sex/gender is defined by the individual's sense of identity rather than biology or society is gaining ground in some quarters, and in some countries, such as Argentina, Canada, Norway and Denmark, legislation has been introduced which makes changing legal gender a very simple process (Ekman 2021, 10). These ideas, however, are not reflected in the advice books in this study, which treat men and women, masculinity and femininity as fixed and stable categories, with fixed behaviours, interests, skills and goals.

Science in the service of culture

Concurrent with ideas of the fluidity of gender and sex, and the social and cultural constructions and negotiations of bodies and identities, there is research conducted focusing on biological differences between men and women. Some of this research is, for example, trying to establish whether heart attacks manifest themselves differently in men and women, or whether male and female bodies react differently to antidepressants (Criado-Perez 2019). The value of this type of research lies in the potentially better health care that women and men may receive. Another strand of research, however, is attempting to find biological reasons for human conduct, for example in the structure of the human brain. In short, scientists are looking for the 'male' brain, the 'female' brain or the 'gay' brain in order to explain what is often sociocultural traits. Psychologist and neuroscientist Cordelia Fine has written an overview and analysis of scientific research relating to sex and gender, *Delusions of Gender* (2010). In this she shows comprehensively, not only how gender stereotypes inform scientific research into, and explanations of, sexual differences between men and women, but also how research intended to establish and confirm biological differences between sexes is used by scientists and journalists to bolster preconceived societal notions of what is typically male or female. Because this type of research promises simple answers to complex questions, findings sometimes make their way into popular ideas of what it means to be a man or woman, and thus into ideas of parenting and may affect the advice given, for example, to single mothers.

In the research Fine has analysed, two specific research areas are repeatedly singled out as explanations of female and male behaviour, aptitudes and desires, which also crop up in the advice books under analysis. These areas are brain structure and hormones, particularly testosterone. As regards brain structure, Fausto-Sterling and Fine both demonstrate that there is very little evidence to suggest the existence of a male or female brain. For example, a study of the brains of 1 400 women and men showed that although there are some sex-based differences, it is not possible to separate the human brain into two discreet categories – into male and female brains (Joel et al. 2015). In over 92 per cent of all people, it is not possible to determine whether the brain belongs to a woman or a man.

A particular part of the brain examined for sex differences is the corpus callosum, connecting tissue between the two brain hemispheres. Fausto-Sterling (2000, 119) details how research into this part of the brain turns it into what Donna Haraway has termed the 'technoscientific body' (1997, 129). According to Haraway, technoscientific bodies, such as, for example, 'the fetus, chip/computer, gene, race' are 'nodes' that send out 'sticky threads' (1997, 129). These sticky threads, Fausto-Sterling writes, 'traverse our gendered world, trapping bits and pieces like newly hung flypaper' and create narratives that explain human existence (2000, 119). Thus, although the corpus callosum is a very difficult subject to study,[1] supposed size differences between women and men have been used to create what Fausto-Sterling terms '[c]allosal narratives', which link 'the underrepresentation of women in science with hormones, patterns of cognition, how best to educate boys and girls, homosexuality, left versus righthandedness, and women's intuition' (2000, 119). In short, the callosal narrative becomes a way of explaining and justifying social structures that privilege men and discriminate against women.

Science seeking to confirm sex differences also looks at other parts of the brain, where activity, or lack thereof, is taken to prove that sociocultural differences, such as the number of women studying mathematics at university, are caused by biology. MRI scans are frequently used to demonstrate these differences, even though MRI analysis studies the brain 'at an interpretive remove' (Fausto-Sterling 2000, 126). The scans do not show neurons firing, actual thought processes taking place, even though this is often claimed when the results are popularized.[2] Instead, the images show comparisons in blood oxygen levels between a baseline when the brain is at rest and when it is carrying out a specific task. These comparisons then result in 'statistical significance at the end of several stages of complicated analysis' (Fine 2010, 135). The complicated analysis means that it is not possible to draw the kinds of conclusions put forward by those who wish to promote discreet sex differences, or as Fine writes, 'there's plenty of scope for spurious findings of sex differences in neuroimaging research' (2010, 135).

The other popular explanation for differences in human conduct is testosterone. Fine, in her book *Testosterone Rex* (2017), traces how hormones are used to explain all manner of behaviours, aptitudes, desires and habits, so that biological sex becomes 'a basic, pervasive, powerful and direct cause of human outcomes' justifying sex inequalities in society (2017, 23, 22). In fact, as she shows comprehensively, testosterone is only a small part of the biological, social and cultural developmental system that affects the growing child. It appears that contrary to popular understanding of the hormone, testosterone is often a *result* of social interactions, rather than their *cause* (2017, 128–158).

The type of research outlined earlier tends to be understood by popular media as proof that human brains and human behaviour are fixed at an early stage. In fact, the human brain is very plastic – it continues to develop throughout a person's life, which makes it difficult to argue that a person's personality is fixed by genetics or exposure to hormones in the womb. As psychologist Rosalind Barnett and media critic Caryl Rivers write in *Same Difference: How Gender Myths Are Hurting Our Relationships, Our Children, and Our Jobs*, even though there are sex differences, they make up a very small part of what makes a human: 'We are all a product of many interacting forces, including our genes, our personalities our environment, and chance' (2005, 12).

An observation that is sometimes repeated but which does not seem to take hold in the popular imagination is that in many instances the differences between individuals within a sex are greater than differences between the sexes (Fine 2017, 91–92). This, for example, was the result of the metastudy conducted by Professor of Psychology Janet Shibley Hyde (2005). She found that most of the expected sex differences between women and men were either non-existent or negligible. More importantly, however, is the fact that although there appears to be sex-based differences in human brains, these differences 'may have little consequence for behavior' (Fine 2017, 93). The question is not why women and men are so different, but how 'sex (usually) creates essentially different reproductive systems, while allowing the differences in men's and women's behaviour to be *non*-essential: overlapping and mosaic, instead of categorically different; conditional on context, not fixed; diverse, rather than uniform' (2017, 179). In short, the question is rather why women and men are so similar.

The biological determinism revealed and critiqued by Fausto-Sterling, Fine, Shibley Hyde and Barnett and Rivers not only continues to inform research questions and guide research but is also very much part of cultural conversations about what it means to be human. It further exerts a very strong influence on attitudes towards childrearing. As noted in the introduction, the trend in childcare has gone from seeing it as childrearing by parents who know what they are doing to parenting by parents who must be monitored or guided, lest they inflict irreparable damage on their offspring (Macvarish 2016, 7). One part of this parenting discourse centres on babies' brains. These are presented as under constant threat from inept parents, who may not only fail to provide the foetus with a 'healthy uterine environment' and later the child with intellectual stimulation, but who may also expose the child to 'toxic stress'; indeed they may even be labelled 'toxic parents' (2016, 14, 34, 31). As Macvarish notes, 'parental culpability is lifelong' (2016, 14). The assumption of fixed gendered natures in children, the resultant claim that parenting should be gendered or the child will be warped for life informs many of the advice books analysed in this study.

Masculinity studies

A main concern of many of the advice books is how the boys can develop the right kind of masculinity without access to a father or other male role model, without specifying explicitly what this kind of masculinity entails. This section will give an overview of how scholars have approached masculinity to provide a context for some of the ways the advice authors position themselves for or against different types of practices, such as what has been called hybrid masculinity, metrosexuality, the New Dad and hegemonic masculinity.

Masculinity scholars C. J. Pascoe and Tristan Bridges specifically ask the question 'What is masculinity?' in the introduction to their edited volume *Exploring Masculinities* (2016a, 1). As they observe, there is a 'notion that everyone knows exactly what we mean' by the term masculinity, yet, when probed further, there are a number of inconsistencies; there is no simple, straightforward answer (2016a, 3). Hence the plural 'masculinities' in the title of the book. Masculinity, they argue, like femininity, is not decided by biology (2016a, 3). Raewyn Connell notes that in 'popular ideology', masculinity is stereotypically assumed to be the result of 'male biology. Men behave the way they do because of testosterone, or big muscles, or a male brain. Accordingly, masculinity is fixed' (2000, 57). However, Connell writes, '[m]en's bodies do not determine the patterns of masculinity'. Rather their 'bodies are addressed, defined and disciplined … and given outlets and pleasures, by the gender order of society' (2000, 12). She notes that '[m]asculinities are created in specific historical circumstances' and when those change 'the gender practices can be contested and reconstructed' (2000, 13–14). Thus masculinities change over time, in response to historical and sociocultural circumstances (Pascoe and Bridges 2016b, 37–38).

Such a response is perhaps what is manifested in what is referred to as 'hybrid masculinities' (Bridges and Pascoe 2019). The term hybrid masculinities is used to describe the 'selective incorporation of identity typically associated with various marginalized and subordinated masculinities, and —at times—femininities into privileged men's gender performances and identities' (2019, 204). Included into hybrid masculinities can be for example metrosexuality or what was termed the 'new dad' in the 1980s and 1990s, as exemplified in sitcoms such as *The Cosby Show* and *Family Ties*. Bridges and Pascoe argue that this should not be assumed to be a change in patriarchal masculinity, but rather as 'expressions of gender and sexual inequality' (2019, 206). Aspects and facets of marginalized identities are appropriated and redefined but still 'reproduce contemporary systems of gendered, race, and sexual inequalities' (2019, 204–205). This is exemplified, for example, in US television news reporting on stay-at-home fathers in the 1990s (Vavrus 2002). In the news, caring for children was redefined as 'properly masculine' (2002, 353). However, as Mary Douglas Vavrus contends, this type of writing did not actually challenge 'more traditional masculine identities depicted in the media'; rather, it 'reinscribe[d] significant aspects of patriarchal privilege within domestic space' (2002, 353). Kristie Rowan Humphreys has found the same type of representation in US TV commercials, which feature 'emotional, domestically competent' fathers, but balance those out with 'hypermasculinized depictions' to compensate for the fact that the fathers are 'working within a historically feminine realm' (2016, 121). As will be seen, hybrid masculinities are acknowledged in some of the advice books, but are usually regarded as a threat to the kind of masculinity that the young boys are expected to achieve.

The kind of masculinity most hinted at in the advice books, even though rarely defined, is the one that aligns most closely with hegemonic masculinity (see e.g. Connell 2000, 2005; Connell and Messerschmidt 2005). This concept refers to the most privileged way of performing masculinity in a given society at a given time. This is not to say that hegemonic masculinity defines a 'specific "type" of man', but 'a configuration of gendered practice within a system of gender relations that is internally contradictory and rife with conflict' (Pascoe and Bridges 2016a, 20). Connell specifically makes it clear that hegemonic masculinity is not a 'fixed character type' even though it has come to be used as such by other critics (2000, 23).

Part of the cultural idea of masculinity as 'fixed' and the valorization of hegemonic masculinity entails that masculinity can be threatened. This is reflected in the consistent concerns over the centuries of the crisis of masculinity (as discussed by, for example, Connell 2000; Griswold 1993; LaRossa 1997). The masculinity of young boys is presented as particularly vulnerable, needing support and protection (Messner 2016, 200). Amongst the forces that threaten young boys are their mothers. As Michele Adams and Scott Coltrane write in their analysis of gender, power and privilege in the family, 'boys are expected to reject their mothers … in order to achieve manhood' (2005, 238). Boys who stay too close to their mothers run the risk of never becoming 'real' men.

Masculinity studies, and in particular the concept of hegemonic masculinity, has come under some criticism in recent years (see e.g. Beasley 2012; 2015; Berggren 2014; Waling 2019).[3] In particular, it has been suggested that the concept is too rigid and that the field of masculinity studies runs the risk of becoming preoccupied with types, not allowing for fluidity of identities (Beasley 2012, 575). Andrea Waling, for instance, has questioned the efficacy of trying to establish a 'typology of masculinit(ies)', such as *'inclusive'*, *'mosaic'* or *'hybrid'* (2019, 94), in order to explain men's behaviours and practices, suggesting that a new type is simply invented to account for practices that do not conform to type. Like, for example, Kalle Berggren, she further advocates a greater focus on agency, rather than on masculinity 'as something that is done to men, or something to which men are victims' (2019, 98). Berggren also warns against 'reify[ing] dominated as well as dominating groups' (2014, 234). These scholars all point to the danger in constructing men as a fixed group, reactively accepting or resisting sociocultural expectations placed on them, rather than as discursively constructed by competing societal discourses. Although I agree with many of their points, in the analysis of the advice books I will make use of Beasley's 'strategic essentialism', treating the gender identity category of men as a 'universalised group identity' (2015, 575). The subject positions of men and boys are not simple, clear-cut or easily defined, but they are treated as such by the advice authors.

The advice authors thus favour 'biological determinism, which emphasizes the body, and sex-role theory, which emphasizes broad cultural expectations' (Connell 2000, 151). They never address concepts such as intersex, trans issues or gender fluidity.[4] As discussed in Chapter 4, there is criticism voiced against aspects of traditional fatherhood, but there is no recognition that the growing boy may be 'positioned by … incompatible but competing discourses' of what it entails to be a man (Berggren 2014, 238).

Gender and Borderwork in the Advice Books

In the late 1970s and early 1980s, sociologist Barrie Thorne conducted a series of studies in schools in California, observing a number of school children at work and play. She noted that in many situations, gender was not an issue. Yet, in other situations, she witnessed how 'gender boundaries' were 'activated' so that the identities as girls and boys eclipsed other identities (1994, 64). The children became more aware of 'gender as a dichotomy' and the children would take up 'antagonistic' positions (1994, 64). Based on these observations, she formulated her theory of borderwork, borrowing the term from Fredrik Barth's analysis of social relations across ethnic boundaries (1994, 64). In Thorne's observations, she saw how the children would slip in and out of different identities, but when gender boundaries were activated, 'situations [would] often teeter between play and aggression, and heterosexual meaning lurk within other definitions' (1994, 66). In these instances, gender would trump all other identities and regulate the children's actions. Thorne's conceptualization of borderwork has been applied by sociologist Andrea Doucet in her study of fathers' caregiving, *Do Men Mother?* (2018). Pondering what triggers gender boundaries between 'girls and boys, men and women, mothers and fathers', she asks the very salient question: 'Who are the gatekeepers at these borders?' (2018, 43).

Drawing on Thorne's and Doucet's work, I use the term 'borderwork' to describe the way the advice books draw attention to and police the supposed borders between mothers and fathers, between mothers and sons. Through a focus on the body, on hormones and on brain structures, social and cultural traits are reduced to a common-sense understanding of gender, which is used to regulate the mother reader and carve out a very restricted niche for her son. In response to Doucet's question, I would argue that the gatekeepers are the authors of the advice books, who, despite their diverse backgrounds, have a vested interest in activating gender boundaries. In many cases, this interest is grounded in traditional values framed by neoliberalism, conservative Christianity and a general sense that US society is falling apart. This will be further discussed in Chapter 3.

In most of the advice books, gender boundaries are invoked and established, often as early as on the cover, where it is implied that the mother reader must struggle with understanding her son (e.g., Moore and Moore 2013; Passley 2006; Phillips 2018; Watkins 2017). This borderwork then continues throughout the books. Thorne's observation indicated that gender boundaries amongst children are 'episodic and ambiguous' and that they can be dismantled as quickly as they are erected (1994, 84). However, the advice books are extended exercises in setting up and maintaining gender borders, attempting to establish a 'sense of cultural difference' (1994, 64). This borderwork is attempted through biological determinism as well as claiming insurmountable cultural dichotomies. By making claims of social injustice directed towards boys and invoking Frank Furedi's 'paranoid parenting' (2008), suggesting that the boys are physically and emotionally vulnerable, the advice books function as gatekeepers, enforcing the borders between mothers and sons, between boys and girls and between mothers and fathers.

Borderwork between mothers (girls) and sons

Since these are advice books generally directed towards single mothers, the books take as the starting point that it is very difficult for such mothers to raise sons. Reasons given for this difficulty include 'financial burdens … endless chores … and the lonely self-doubt and despair' (Bromfield and Erwin 2001, xiii) as well as 'feelings of inadequacy' (Panettieri 2008, 79). But the books also comfort the mother reader by claiming that the fundamental difference between boys and girls is responsible for many of the mother's problems: 'Boys do behave differently' (Engber and Klungness 2006, 276). It is not the mother's fault that she is struggling. As Meeker explains, the 'mother-son dyad is complicated by the opposition of gender. Neither mother nor son can fully understand what it is like to be the other half of the equation' (2015, xv). Not only does gender make it difficult for mother and son to understand each other, but the differences go so much deeper than that; they are so different that they can be regarded as a 'very different species', Meeker contends (2015, 71) Gina Panettieri's co-writer, psychologist Philip Hall uses a similar explanation: boys' thoughts and actions are 'completely alien to a female … they're different from you, in so many ways' (18). This attitude absolves the mother of any blame; it is biology that causes the problems. In this way, the advice books do borderwork by constructing an unbridgeable gap between mothers and sons. Through the imagery of aliens and different species, it is made clear that it is impossible for mothers to understand and adequately provide for their sons on their own.

In their attempts to establish the biological difference between boys and their mothers, authors often refer both to nature and to science. One of the ways in which science is evoked is through computer metaphors. Terms such as 'hardwired' or 'wired' are used to explain why boys behave in ways their mothers do not like (for instance Allen and Dickerson 2012, 22; Biddulph 2015, preface; Dennis 2015, 149; Krause 2014, 122; Meeker 2015, 226; Panettieri 2008, 42). Science is also brought in through references to MRI and PET scans, which are used as 'biological evidence' that boys and girls are fundamentally different (Bromfield and Erwin 2001, 24). References to differences in the corpus callosum (Fausto-Sterling's 'callosal narrative'), boys' supposedly underdeveloped prefrontal cortex and other claims about major differences between male and female brains are also used to explain why boys are different (e.g., Biddulph 2015, 66; Elium and Elium 2004, 11; Panettieri 2008, 19). Endocrinology is invoked and testosterone is presented as the guiding force in a boy's life: he is 'under the spell of the masculine biological plan' (Elium and Elium 2004, 13, see also, for example, Biddulph 2015; Engber and Klungness 2006; Bryant 2015).

These appeals to science reflect how neuropsychiatric research is making headway into parenting, as neuroparenting (Macvarish 2016). The neuroparenting and 'recent discoveries about boys' development are yoked with 'age-old wisdom' about what is simply nature (Bromfield and Erwin 2001, xiii). For example, when explaining that boys have much more energy compared to girls, nature is invoked: 'That's how they are built' (2001, 18). In fact, insisting that boys 'sit and be quiet' is 'pushing them away from their natural inclinations and trying to make them something they are not' (Joyce 2018, 80). Other innate traits make boys bad at listening, bad at thinking ahead and bad at recognizing emotions in other people (Panettieri 2008, 19). As Bromfield and Erwin write: 'Boys don't have nearly as much capacity as girls do to speak before doing and to think before saying' (2001, 23). Boys are also bad at persevering with tasks that are boring or do not give immediate satisfaction. All of these traits put them on a collision course with their mothers, who are constructed differently, for example, 'lacking their sons' inborn love of noise' (2001, 21). This is brought up by a number of authors, such as Elium and Elium (2004), Meeker (2015), Biddulph (2015) and Krause (2014). Some of the books have subtitles that reiterate the idea that boys drive their mothers insane, promising to 'save your sanity' (for instance, Krause 2014). Thus through the merging of science and nature, the son is constructed as an alien species, whom the mother cannot truly understand.

Borderwork is also carried out through the stereotype that men are taciturn and women talk too much. This is transposed onto boys and their supposed reluctance to talk to their mothers. It is stated as a commonplace that it is unnatural for boys to talk – about what they did in school, how sports practice went or their emotions. As Meeker explains, 'girls are communicators and most boys aren't' (2015, 8). Since mothers are hardwired to talk a great deal (2015, 28), they need to learn to leave the boys alone and not insist on probing. In fact, Panettieri brings up mothers' need for talk as a point of potential danger to their sons. She paints a picture of the mother pursuing the unwilling boy through the house, wanting to 'talk out the problem, which turns out to only make the situation worse!' (2008, 160). The mother reader is told not to expect a son to be like a daughter, who is very happy to share all her thoughts and emotions with her mother (for instance Allen and Dickerson 2012, 18; Panettieri 2008, 10).

Added to the supposed biological fact that boys cannot talk to their mothers, they are also unable to listen. It is futile to tell them to do things, it is claimed, because boys will not take heed. Panettieri offers a medical explanation also for this, referencing research which suggests that boys cannot hear voices in the female range as well as in the male range (2008, 20–23).[5] Similarly, Biddulph quotes Australian research which suggests that 25 per cent of six-year-old children find it difficult to process what they hear into separate words, and 70 per cent of those children are boys (2015, 14). This is then taken as evidence that boys in general have trouble understanding adults. Added to these biological difficulties is boys' inability to learn things through verbal instruction. According to, for example Allen and Dickerson, boys only learn by watching someone do something (2012, 19).

Some of the authors are aware that their attempts to explain differences between boys and girls may be read as sexist and reactionary. They attempt to forestall criticism by noting that what they are saying is not popular and not politically correct, but it has to be said nonetheless. Phillips, for example, states that his book 'dares to go beyond the surface of political correctness' in order to save the 'millions of single mothers' from making the mistakes they have made until now (2018, blurb). Bromfield and Irwin write that '[p]olitically correct or not, boy's brains do differ from girls' brains in structure, function, and chemistry' (2001, 24). Others are careful to state that they are not saying that all boys are this way – they are aware that children come in all sorts of varieties (Allen and Dickerson 2012; Biddulph 2015) but that they will simply write about the most common generalities. Some books claim to want to dispel the myths and stereotypes of gender differences (Panettieri 2008), only to end up reinforcing them, whereas, for example, Bromfield and Erwin write that the assumptions of 'generations of folk wisdom' have now been 'confirmed' by contemporary research (2001, 16). In short, the general message in the advice books is that traditional stereotypes are correct and that this is now supported through scientific research: there is an unbridgeable, biological gap between mothers and sons.

Borderwork between boys and girls

In the process of setting up and policing the borders between mothers and sons, the advice books also set boys up as more vulnerable than girls. It is presented as a given that 'boys' brains are less well equipped for impulse control, social skills and understanding, and language' (Bromfield and Erwin, 2001, 24). Panettieri claims that boys have 'weaker neural connections in the temporal lobe region' than girls do, which would explain why their 'listening skills', ability to detect 'cues by tone of voice' and their 'detailed memory storage' are developing so much more slowly than those of girls (2008, 19). Paradoxically, the same callosal narratives that are used to justify, for instance, gendered pay gaps, lack of women in STEM research and unequal distribution of housework are here used to represent boys as vulnerable and disadvantaged in comparison to girls.

This representation of boys also extends to school. Many of the 'backlash' books mentioned in the introduction repeat the claim that boys mature more slowly than girls: Sax, for example, writes that 'girls' development is roughly 2 years ahead of the boys' (2016, 20). Several of the advice authors make similar claims, arguing that boys are anything between six months and two years behind girls in their development by the time they start school. Some authors therefore argue that boys should start school later. Biddulph, for example, recommends waiting a year, allowing the boys' 'fine-motor skills and cognitive skills' to develop (2015, 148).

There is another side to the discussion, however. Some of the authors choose to view boys' experiences in school in light of the debate concerning 'boys' underachievement' (Titus 2004, 145), particularly in comparison with girls (Skelton and Francis 2009, 103). In this debate, boys are presented as '"victims"', 'specifically of single (fatherless) families, female-dominated primary schooling, and feminism which has enabled girls' successes' (Skelton 2001, 6). Feminist teachers are said to disapprove of and punish 'boys' natural masculinity' (Titus 2004, 150), and schools have been changed so that they 'are set up for girls to succeed and boys to fail', through the 'practice and delivery of the curriculum, management strategies and teacher expectations' which all 'favour girls' (Skelton 2002, 87–88). As Skelton has observed, the problems with boys alleged underachievement in school are often traced to three areas: numbers, school culture and a feminist backlash. According to this argumentation, there are too few male teachers in school, the school environment favours girls and the feminist movement has created inequalities in schools so that boys are discriminated against (2002, 6). All of these understandings are repeated in the advice books. Antonio Anderson, for example, claims that the 'lack of male teachers' in the early years of school cause boys 'to lose their creativity' since 'they have no male influence to cultivate that in them' (2017, 8). Dennis writes that boys struggle in 'an educational system that is not catering to their needs' (2015, 82). Some of those needs are described by Bromfield and Erwin: 'Boys can't read their own chicken-scratch writing; they punch and kick out their feelings, punch and kick out their interpersonal conflicts, need to get outside and burn off excess energy, and fall out of their chairs a lot' (2001, 222–223). Panettieri tells the reader to be concerned about whether her child's school has 'boy-friendly subjects', including 'books and stories that would interest a male reader' (2008, 166).

One of the major concerns for many of the authors, however, is the unfair treatment they claim boys receive at the hands of female teachers. Dennis states that boys are 'punished … for being boisterous and disruptive' (2015, 82). Allen and Dickerson maintain that female teachers reward 'feminine behavior in boys (sitting quietly and exhibiting non-assertive behaviour)', 'punish boys for being aggressive in the classroom or on the playground during recess' and 'give girls higher grades' for work of the same standard (2012, 73–74). Panettieri writes that boys are unfairly 'judged relative to a standard of female behavior and abilities' (23). She also references an unnamed 'specialist in male behaviour' claiming that boys 'are being treated like defective girls' (167).

In short, school is often presented as a hostile environment for boys, where they are set up to fail, partly by the schools themselves and partly by their innate resistance to school work. However, although never stated explicitly, many of the authors appear to subscribe to the view that to willingly do homework, to excel in school without being forced to by parents, is effeminate. There is overall something paradoxical about the way for example Biddulph, Meeker, Allen and Dickerson and Panettieri write about pre-pubescent and teenage boys. On the one hand the boys are presented as clumsy, inattentive, loud and accident-prone, which is framed as something akin to a disability. On the other hand, these supposedly innate characteristics are also framed as admirable. The boys are not docile, reliable, quiet and hardworking like girls, but, the authors almost seem to be saying, that is exactly what makes girls boring and boys exciting. As Adams and Coltrane write, the 'cultural concept of masculinity is based on a proscription against being feminine' (2005, 232) and the advice book authors, while on the one hand seemingly complaining about boys' tendency, for instance, to break things and lie to get out of doing homework, valorize them for the same qualities, since they make them not feminine.

Borderwork between Mothers and Fathers

The borderwork between fathers and (single) mothers rests on the claim that the latter are not capable to raise boys on their own. Their lack of knowledge, coupled with a general unsuitability for dealing with sons beyond toddlerhood may lead to irreparable harm, not only to the individual child but to the whole world. Advice author William Small writes, for example: 'The greatest social, cultural, and financial problem plaguing every nation across the globe is fatherlessness' (2017, x). This is hyperbole, of course, but it is a claim made by a variety of commentators. As Macvarish notes in regards to the 'early years movement', which argues for early intervention into children's lives, poor parenting on an individual level is presented as a danger to society (2016, 11). Small's claim is repeated, for example, by 'backlash' authors Farrell and Gray, who write that there is a 'worldwide decline among our sons', a boy crisis that is caused by 'dad-deprived boys' (2018, 4, 103). These dad-deprived boys 'hurt us—physically, psychologically and economically' in a wide variety of ways, including carrying out school shootings and joining ISIS (2018, 106). Here the borderwork is displayed in its perhaps starkest form. The young boys are dad-deprived, but it is the mother's inability to make up for that deprivation that makes her a danger to her son, and by extension, to the rest of society, as will be shown.

The pathogenic mother

To set the stage for the advice given, a great many of the authors begin by listing all the threats against the fatherless boy. These boys are more likely than others to fall prey to illness, drug abuse, alcoholism, depression and suicide. They are more likely to experiment with unsafe sex and reckless driving, and they are also more likely to drop out of school. Fatherless boys 'experience more accidental injury, asthma, frequent headaches, and speech defects' as well as schizophrenia (Allen and Dickerson 2012, 141, 142). Further, because women have a higher pain threshold, they 'under-evaluate their son's discomfort', 'ignor[ing] early symptoms of disease' which may lead to more serious illnesses (2012, 141). Additionally, fatherless boys go through puberty at a later age (Joyce 2018, 16). Very little substantial evidence is given for these claims, and little or no allowance is made for other socioeconomic factors such as poverty. The intention is to create a feeling of urgency and inadequacy in the mother reader so that she will be receptive to the advice given by the authors. Allen and Dickerson, for example, on the back cover of their book ask the prospective reader whether she knows 'the 5 major diseases and ailments that your son is more likely to acquire without his father' (2012). The borderwork here is to convince the mother reader that her son is in danger for his life if he grows up without a father.[6]

In addition to the health problems she may create, the single mother is also likely to endanger her son mentally, or as Meeker phrases it, mothers must take care not to 'cripple our sons emotionally' (2015, 160). Mothers cripple their sons by, for instance, shouting at them, shaming them in front of their friends (e.g., Anderson 2017, 14), or treating them like 'verbal punching bags' (Estelle 2013, 4). Mothers are told that they are too hard on their sons, using harsh language that takes away their self-esteem and has 'long-term implications on [their] success' (Phillips 2018, 45). Yet, they are also told, sometimes by the same authors, that they are too soft on their sons: 'it is said that we love our sons and raise our daughters' (Howland 2020, 21; Phillips 2018, 15). Rick Johnson writes that '[f]emales can destroy healthy masculinity' by shielding their boys from life's difficulties (2011, 100). The authors suggest that mothers teach daughters how to fend for themselves but spoil their sons by waiting on them hand and foot whilst allowing them to be disrespectful in words and actions (Anderson 2017, 5; Lewis 2010, 48), permitting them to watch television for hours on end (Allen and Dickerson 2012, 113), not demanding that they help out at home (Bromfield and Erwin 2001, 121) and spending far too much money on them (Anderson 2017, 4; King 2015, 41). In short, mothers are simultaneously too strict and too soft, and this endangers their sons.

Mothers are also a threat when they overstep emotional boundaries, creating what some backlash commentators have called 'mother-enmeshed men' (Adams 2007), an outcome of the so-called 'emotional incest syndrome' (Love 1990). The solution to this is to break up the 'mother-son dynamic' (Lee 2015). These books evidence the cultural fear that mothers will become too emotionally invested in their sons, and this is reflected in the advice books. Not only do they advise against calling small boys 'the man of the house', but they also present as a very real threat the mother who treats her teenage son as a boyfriend to the extent that some men are in effect 'dating their moms' (Anderson 2017, 38). Some of the authors even hint at sexual improprieties, as is discussed in the next chapter. This is why it is so important that sons take 'the journey over the bridge … from Mother to Father' (Elium and Elium 2004, 20). If they do not, they will be 'unclear about a man's role and identity in the world' (2004, 20). In short, the mother is constructed as a danger her son must distance himself from.

A mother cannot be a father

The borderwork, gatekeeping, evidenced in the books accumulates into a message across the literature that a mother is not able to be a father. Many of the authors write that a mother cannot do the job of two people (for instance Moore and Moore 2013; Tardy 2006), but it is also claimed that she cannot be a father, doing a father's things, such as teaching the boy 'how to change tires, fix leaking pipes or hit baseballs' (King 2015, 5). Some authors stress very emphatically that '[o]nly men can raise boys to be men' (Anderson 2017, viii). Elium and Elium maintain that 'mothers make lousy fathers' (2004, 89). Allen and Dickerson even go so far as to suggest that trying to take over what is the father's job, such as playing sports with the boy, is 'one of the most damaging things a mother can do' (2012, 65), since it makes the boy a target for bullying.

One area in which fathers are said to excel and mothers fail is in physical and emotional toughness. Fathers roughhouse with their children (Joyce 2018, 18), and they give them healthy competition, which 'prepare[s] them for a world in which winning is more important than avoiding hurt feelings' (Allen and Dickerson 2012, 24). Fathers are not concerned when boys push and shove, realizing that a boy needs to learn to take a bit of teasing 'without getting his feelings hurt', that he needs to "man up" (Dennis 2015, 66). Mothers find it difficult to 'understand boys' different ways of interacting' (Panettieri 2008, 42). This supposed toughness also gives fathers the necessary strength to push their sons to achieve things. A mother will try to protect her son from the pain of failure, which means that she is 'creating a man who will be an emotional cripple, handicapped by his own fear' (Bourne Jr 2016, 69). It also takes a father to make a boy obey and carry out his tasks without complaint (Stoppe 2013, 116–117). In addition, it is reiterated that the single mother does not have the biological or cultural knowledge to raise a boy. Specifically, she has never had an erection (Dennis 2015, 28; Howland 2020, 20). Matters such as how to shave or how to behave in a men's room are constructed as intensely problematic (Joyce 2018, 33; Howland 2020, 20). As can be deduced from the examples mentioned earlier, what is at stake here is not actually the individual examples, but the borderwork. For the advice authors, it is imperative to show that mothers do not have what it takes to raise a boy to be a man.

Teaching Masculinity in the Advice Books

The family is where boys learn about the privilege that comes with being male and 'the ways in which male privilege equates to power' (Adams and Coltrane 2005, 233). Privilege and power seem to form part of the core of what the advice authors regard as masculinity, and the main problem in most of the advice books is that single mothers cannot teach their sons masculinity. They may 'celebrate it' (Bromfield and Erwin 2001, 183), but they cannot model it or teach it. In Lisa Norwood's words, a single mother cannot be a 'positive male role model' (2016, back cover). A fatherless boy will not 'observe healthy masculine traits' (Meeker 2015, 80), and he will not take on the 'masculine role he was created to be in' (Joyce 2018, 78). Boys need men to 'show them what true manhood is all about' (Dennis 2015, 37). Words such as *masculinity* and *manhood* abound in the books, but they are rarely defined beyond examples such as that men are put on this earth to be leaders, particularly of their families (Dennis 2015; Krause 2014) and that they have a 'natural inclination' to protect women (Dennis 2015, 125). Protection of the family is also one of the core aspects of Johnson's vision of manhood (2011, 98). Bourne Jr defines masculinity by what it is *not*, 'aggressiveness, strength, and callousness', but he gives no definition of what it *is* (2016, 82).

The books could be read as an extended exercise in trying to pin down what masculinity really is. Some authors try to define it in terms of nouns and adjectives, as qualities, such as *responsibility, honour, pride, respect, discipline, self-control, sports* and *competitiveness*. Small gives a list of 15 'essential elements of manhood' which include 'integrity, excellence, bravery' (103). Others define it in terms of knowledge or actions. Joyce has compiled a list of 18 '"man skill" essentials' that a young man must learn. These are 'skills a man needs to learn, according to other men', and they include personal hygiene, car maintenance, as well as cooking, taking care of a baby and handling a job interview (Joyce, 2018, 63–64). For, others, such as Allen and Dickerson, masculinity means carrying out what Douglas Schrock and Michael Schwalbe refer to as 'manhood acts' (2009). To Allen and Dickerson, masculinity is taught to the boy by involving him in masculine tasks such as fishing, hunting and buying a boat (2012, 134). Masculinity thus seems to either consist of skills or personality traits that everyone should have, such as the ability to fill up one's car or be responsible and trustworthy, or it is made up of acts that may be viewed as gendered masculine, but of course are also carried out and enjoyed by women, such as camping or playing baseball. In short, the masculinity constructed in the books, although presented as something which everyone agrees on, turns out to be quite illusive. When discussed, it is of the traditional variety, drawing on the hegemonic masculinity that is seen as having existed in the 1950s. Many of the authors discuss the importance of teaching sons how to respect their future wives and be good fathers, but this is couched in terms of traditional courtship, opening doors and pulling out chairs. Not much is said concerning actual fathering, and none of the authors bring up anything to do with nurturance. This reflects Nancy Dowd's observation that there is no value placed on nurturing in traditional masculinity (2000, 11).

The construction of masculinity in the advice books highlights its paradox. On the hand masculinity is a biological fact, something that is innate and hardwired, which would suggest that it is universal and inevitable. On the other hand, it is something that must be taught, which leaves it open to threat. Meeker writes that it is vital for the little boy's 'ego development' that he is allowed to see his father as stronger than his mother. If she is the stronger party, it 'threatens his masculinity' since he models his own adult self on his father (2015, 160–161). One of the informants Dennis has interviewed talks about how his uncles taught him that it was not permissible to play with his female cousins' dolls: "'hold up – that's not for you – that's for them (the girls!)'" (2015, 125). Elium and Elium, grounded in the mythopoeic men's movement and quoting from Robert Bly's *Iron Hans*, devote an entire chapter to how 'Men are made, not born'.

If masculinity is not inculcated successfully in the boys, they will not grow up to be successful men. This shows up in a variety of ways. Allen and Dickerson write about what they call 'Unfriendly World Children', 'who invariably see the world as an unfriendly place with potential for great harm' and who may 'grow up to become ticking time bombs' such as Ted Bundy and Saddam Hussein (2012, 9, 10). Dennis uses the term 'MRW', men raised by women (2015). Such men lack 'masculine perspectives and development', which may manifest itself in not minding earning less than one's wife and being comfortable with strong women (2015, 10, 74). MRWs tend to be metrosexuals, according to Dennis, 'focusing on clothing and appearance in a manner more like a woman than a man' (2015, 76). These MRWs and Unfriendly World Children are thus not only slightly ridiculous but also potentially dangerous to society.

Men who have not had access to the right kind of masculinity will also fail to exhibit the right kind of masculine restraint: they will be 'more emotional than rational' (Dennis 2015, 10), to 'overact' (Allen and Dickerson 2012, 156). They will find it difficult to form friendships with men and instead have 'numerous female friends' (2012, 155). The reason why advice authors present this as problematic may be found in Doucet's findings that hegemonic masculinity proscribes close emotional relationships between men as well as between men and women who are not their sexual partners (2018, 151–153). For a man to have close friendships with women or want to have emotional closeness with other men is to fail to conform to traditional expectations of masculinity.

Since the single mother cannot model or teach masculinity, she needs the father to do that, or find some other male role model to do it. As Anna Tarrant et al. note, it is a very common claim in popular debates that boys need 'positive male role models' if they are to 'grow into healthy and well-adjusted men and fathers', even though there is little empirical evidence to suggest that this is the case (2015, 60, 71). This claim is also made in many of the advice books. The authors write that boys 'look to their father regarding how to treat women, their work ethic, and many other areas men need to be guided in' (Joyce 2018, 50). Not only is it in their 'nature … to reserve their greatest reverence for other men, not women' (Bryant 2015, 28), but they will only learn through 'watching other males' (Allen and Dickerson 2012,

18). They simply will not learn from women. So if there is no father around to teach the boy, another suitable male role model must be found. He can be a male relative, a sports coach, a teacher or a priest/rabbi/minister (for instance Anderson 2017, 26; Bourne Jr 2016, 84; Bromfield and Erwin 2001, 248; Dennis 2015, 33; Jones 2015, 8; Meeker 2015, 22).

It should be noted that what is discussed here is not the question that it is difficult for a single person to raise children and that it would work better with two adults. It is made clear by some of the authors that two women in a household does not count. For example, as noted earlier, to Allen and Dickerson, lesbian relationships count as single-mother households, since there is no man present (2012). Similarly, households comprising mother and grandmother are insufficient for the needs of growing boy, since again, there is no man around (Dennis 2015). The young boy needs to have the 'profound, numinous power of the masculine soul ... acknowledged, nurtured, and honored' (Elium and Elium 2004, 30). This is not possible without access to other men. What is at stake in these suggestions for a male role model is thus masculinity. It is assumed that there is only one kind, and this is at the same time innate and stable and under threat, needing to be developed and protected.

Heteronormativity in the Advice Books

A heteronormative view of family

The preferred family structures that are referenced in the advice books do not reflect the diverse family structures discussed by Casper and Bianchi (2002) and Golombok (2015). With very few exceptions, the books present traditional families as the ideal, where all children need access to a mother and a father (Leman 2006). Some of the authors do suggest the involvement of an extended family: Panettieri states that uncles, grandfathers and other relatives afford more role models than one father, which is better if the father is not suitable. Howland introduces four mentors for her son, one of which is the boy's uncle. But even these authors assume that everybody wants to get married to a partner of the opposite sex and settle down. There is no room for other family structures. Those authors who are single mothers have either remarried, or make a point of stating that they are hoping to remarry, once they find the right partner.

The threat of sexuality

There is very little discussion of the boys' sexuality in the books and usually when it is brought up, it is in terms of a threat. This threat can come in the form of abuse from adult strangers (Panettieri 2008, 36–38), family members, teachers and priests (Bolds 2008, 185), older boys (Meeker 2015, 228) or girls (Howland 2020, 59). Overall, if girls are mentioned at all, they are represented as seductive threats to the young boys, with their 'tight shirts and short skirts' (Howland 2020, 23) and as 'aggressors' (Anderson 2017, 22). The threat can also take the form of the boys' experimenting with unsafe sex, resulting in STDs or unwanted pregnancies (Meeker 2015, 27; Bourne 2016, 89). Several authors advocate encouraging celibacy (for instance Chisholm 2007; Panettieri 2008). Authors also bring up the embarrassment and difficulty in talking to the boy about sexual matters (Howland 2020). Sexuality is rarely, if ever, addressed as something positive.

Compulsory heterosexuality

The default assumption of the authors is that the sons of the mother readers are heterosexual. Some take pride in their own sons' attractiveness to women (Howland 2020, 180; Watkins 2017, 137). The authors write about how to handle the boy's budding interest in girls, how to teach him how to behave on a date and take for granted that he will marry a woman (Bromfield and Erwin 2001, 2; Krause 2014, 7). Monica Swanson even suggests teaching small boys to pray for their future wives (2019, 184). However, some of the books also address the possibility that the son will turn out to be homosexual. When they do, it is framed in terms of pathology, or as a threat facing the young boy (Bryant 2015, 80–82).

Instead of treating same-sex desire as simply one form of sexuality, many of the books touch on the long-standing cultural fear that too close maternal ties and a lack of male role models will make a boy homosexual (see for instance Panettieri 2008, 25). Sometimes the connection is made explicit, and presented as a sign of weakness, or lack of moral fibre, as in a comment by one of Dennis' informants. He maintains that the '"tremendous amounts of homosexuality"' he, as a corrections officer, has encountered in the prison system is a direct result of the prisoners being raised by single mothers (2015, 130). Bromfield and Erwin also present homosexuality as a weakness. They seemingly refute the claim that close maternal ties lead to homosexuality, writing that a 'mother's healthy love does not create wimpy or homosexual boys' (2001, 194). Thus a mother's *unhealthy* love might cause homosexuality, which they equate with a lack of masculinity, with wimpiness. Should it transpire that the boy is homosexual, they give the mother reader advice on how to help the boy accept his 'disappointing lot in life' (2001, 197). Panettieri, on the other hand, notes that there 'seems to be evidence that in-utero hormone exposure of male fetuses may influence sexual orientation' (2008, 96), reassuring the mother that she is not to blame.

Other authors approach the subject more obliquely, such as Allen and Dickerson, who prefer the term 'gender issues' (2012, 67). They still contend that such issues are problematic, suggesting that they might develop in boys 'not having a male role model' and that this may lead to suicide (2012, 67). Bromfield and Erwin state that 'more mothers are raising boys who are confused about their gender identity, boys who worry about whether they are heterosexual, homosexual, or somewhere betwixt the two' (2001, 190). Like Allen and Dickerson, Bromfield and Erwin seem to confuse same-sex preferences with effeminacy and 'gender confusion' (2001, 197). They give advice on when to put the child in therapy, assuming that 'a heterosexual boy's identity is still possible', and recommend that a therapist advise mothers on 'how much to push his *boy*ness and how much to discourage or indulge his *girl*ness' (2001, 197, original emphasis). To Bromfield and Erwin, homosexuality is the same as gender dysphoria. Thus, like other authors, they discuss homosexuality as a pathological condition to be avoided or managed, possibly tolerated, but never celebrated.

A very small number of authors address the fact that boys may turn out to be homosexual but tend to skate over the issue very quickly in the discussions of rules about dating girls, how to talk about contraceptives, hygiene and similar issues. Only two authors deal with homosexuality in depth. Panettieri has a section titled 'If Your Son Is Gay'. She stresses that it is nothing to worry about, particularly since it is 'hardwired into a child even before birth', and the child's sexual orientation should be 'accepted and supported, and never treated with scorn, rejection, or derision' (2008, 68). But even to her, same-sex preferences are to be tolerated rather than celebrated. Similarly, Denise Bolds has a section called 'Sexual Preferences and the Black Son', which begins with the statement that her son is not a homosexual (2008, 188). The message of the section is that the mother reader should not judge her son but protect him from the judgement of others. Homophobia, '[s]peculation, alienation and hostility can kill your black son' (2008, 190). Still, she links homosexuality to sexual abuse and urges the mother reader to make sure this has not happened (2008, 190). Like Panettieri, Bolds presents same-sex desire as something to be tolerated. The mother reader is encouraged to teach her son to take 'precautions in sexual activity, where he socializes and with whom' (2008, 190). This holds true for any kind of sexual encounter, of course, but the difference in attitudes is striking. Whereas many of the advice authors express hopes for the young men finding loving wives, no one expresses such sentiments regarding same-sex partners. The authors do not envisage homosexual sons finding love and happiness.

The advice books do not give mothers and sons much room to manoeuvre in the roles afforded to them. The mothers are constructed as physically and emotionally very different from their sons. Many books stress that although mothers love their sons, they have very little hope of really understanding them. They are also cautioned that they may very well damage them, not only emotionally but also physically. Similarly, the roles afforded to the sons are also very circumscribed. They are presented as naturally uninterested in reading and learning, but very keen on loud, vigorous, dirty and dangerous activities. As Panettieri writes: 'Boys are exhilarated by physical challenges and thrilled by risks' (2008, 185). There is no room for the boy who loves to read, who prefers quiet play to wrestling, just as there is little room for the boy who feels attracted to other boys, and who does not wish to marry a woman when he grows up.

Chapter 3

CLASS AND RACE: EXPECTATIONS OF MOTHERS AND SONS

The previous chapter analysed the advice books with a focus on gender. Doing so makes it possible to analyse the ways the books reiterate and support cultural ideas about masculinity and femininity, about what it means to be a man or a woman, and what is expected of the growing boy. However, a focus solely on gender gives the impression that the books are homogenous, that they all represent mothers, fathers and sons in the same way. But, as Sharon Hays has pointed out, a mother's approach to mothering is influenced by many different factors, such as 'her class position, race, ethnic heritage, religious background, political beliefs, sexual preferences, physical abilities or disabilities, citizenship status, participation in various subcultures, place of residence, workplace environment, formal education' (1996, 76). This is also evident in the advice books analysed here. The authors, in addition to their gender, come from different racial, class and educational backgrounds, and their intended readership is addressed, implicitly or explicitly, along race and class lines.

This chapter will thus take an intersectional approach, expanding the analysis to include race and class. This will allow for more complex readings, in order to highlight and explore the diversity amongst the books. At a first glance, they all seem to be the same: advice books aimed at single mothers raising sons. But when analysed from the point of view of race and class, their other concerns, strategies, assumptions, expectations and prejudices come to the surface. The single mother is constructed in different ways, depending on whether she is Black or White, working or middle class, and the aims and goals for the growing boys turn out to be different – individual happiness, fulfilling an expected destiny of success or becoming a valued, productive member of a community. When focusing on the added perspectives, the differences between the ways the books shape the reading subject are highlighted.

Intersectionality

In their book *Intersectionality*, Patricia Hill Collins and Sirma Bilge (2020) demonstrate how intersectionality as an analytic tool allows the scholar to study 'a range of social problems' moving beyond seeing people 'as a homogenous, undifferentiated mass of individuals' (2020, 4, 19). In this chapter, I identify which race and class markers the books present and analyse how these affiliations affect the types of advice given, which problem areas are discussed and the ways in which the mother readers are addressed, as well as the social problems that some of the books avoid addressing, such as maternal poverty. Using intersectionality as a 'framework for explaining how categories of race, class, gender, age, and citizenship status, among others, position people differently in the world', the books' heterogeneity becomes apparent (Collins and Bilge 2020, 19).

It has been argued that the scholar should use a truly intersectional perspective – not just tack one or two perspectives on to an existing one. Collins and Bilge, for example, critique how 'class-only explanations treat race, gender, sexuality, dis/ability, and ethnicity as secondary add-ons, namely, as ways to describe the class system more accurately' (2020, 20). In some ways, this is what I am doing: using class and race as add-ons in order to better describe and analyse the gendered cultural attitudes the advice books exhibit. Yet, at the same time, these add-ons demonstrate the differences in advice given to Black or White single mothers, and that this advice intersects with class, demonstrating without acknowledging, for example, the racialized and gendered wealth gap pointed to by Collins and Bilge (2020, 20). An intersectional analysis thus highlights the ways in which these books naturalize and make invisible the financial disparities between single mothers and fathers, as well as between Black and White single mothers.

Race

Race and ethnicity are highly contested concepts (Caliendo and McIlwain 2021a; Spencer 2014). It has been demonstrated again and again that there is no biological foundation for the concept of race (Caliendo and McIlwain 2021b, 1) and for some researchers acknowledging the fact that there are socially constructed differences, dependent on physical differences, is problematic: 'the very term [racism] has come to connote any considerations of race at all' (2021b, 15). Although race and ethnicity are now generally viewed as social constructs, they do have profound effects on people's lived experiences, or as Stephen M. Caliendo and Charlton McIlwain write in *The Routledge Companion to Race and Ethnicity*, 'race and ethnicity, as an experience, are more salient for some than others' (2021b, 2). This is borne out by the advice books under study, where some authors make race the central focus (e.g., Estelle 2013) whereas others do not mention it at all (e.g., Chisholm 2007).

How to address race and ethnicity is not straightforward – scholars approach the concepts from various viewpoints, and one scholar's race is another scholar's ethnicity. As Caliendo and McIlwain note, '[s]ince "race" is not "real" in the sense that it is not a valid biological classification, the construction of race and ethnicity is inherently blurry' (2021b, 2). They and the other contributors to the volume construe race as a 'social construction rooted in physical differences, among the most prominent of which is skin color/tone, and ethnicity [as] centered largely on geographical origin of one's ancestors and/or shared cultural elements' (2021b, 2). Stephen Spencer, on the other hand, in *Race and Ethnicity: Culture, Identity and Representation*, suggests a greater complexity, pointing to how ethnicity may be 'taken to be a more inclusive and less objectifying concept indicating the constantly negotiated nature of boundaries between ethnic groups rather than the essentialism implicit in divisions of "race"' (2014, 55). Added to these blurred boundaries are other political concerns, as well as the geographical location of the scholars themselves. Caliendo and McIlwain write from a US perspective, but Spencer, who works in Britain, notes how the terms race and ethnicity are sometimes used interchangeably, particularly in Europe, and that ethnicity is often regarded as simply a more polite term for race (2014, 41). Yet, using 'ethnicity' in this way can also simply be a way of avoiding the issue, a refusal to address difficult questions and, in doing so, tacitly reify them.

In this study, I will use the terminology used by the authors themselves. In the advice books the terms 'race', 'Black' and 'African American' are used, and I will do the same. I will further capitalize the terms Black and White, although not all authors do so, in order to highlight the 'semiotic struggle [which shows] the power relationship that play[s] out in the official naming of groups' (Spencer 2014, 62). Capitalizing Black puts the term on the same level as, for example, Hispanic American, and capitalizing White brings to the forefront the fact that this is also a racial category. As Spencer points out, Whiteness is usually 'exnominated', 'taken for granted, assumed as natural … not named' (2014, xxiv), what Walton and Caliendo refer to as 'race neutral' (2021, 12).

This race neutrality is prevalent in all the advice books that can be attributed to White authors and assessed as aimed at a White readership, through cover imagery, author pictures and author websites. The material presented is structured and presented as if the content is universal and applies to everyone, even though it is highly inflected not only with race but also class. White authors do not discuss race, possibly because such a race 'is often perceived as nonexistent' (Caliendo and McIlwain 2021b, 2). It could be argued that the authors display the position noted by Hazel Rose Markus and Paula M. L. Moya in their book *Doing Race*: 'Race isn't relevant to me' (2010, 11). The sole exception is Bay Buchanan, but her only comments on race are references to statistics on Black single mothers and their sons' problems in school (2012, 32, 39). Throughout the rest of her book, race is not addressed at all, and she does not refer to herself and her sons as members of a racial category. Thus Whiteness is exonominated in all of the books.

I would argue that most of these advice books are examples of White privilege, a term referring to advantages that are 'not a product of any individual effort or ability but are built into the structure of society' (Jensen 2021, 30). The authors give advice, prescribe actions and assume outcomes that generally pertain to White middle-class people only, but never address them as such. For example, White author Gina Panettieri, concerned with what she sees as the educational system failing boys, and particularly sons of single mothers, urges the mother reader to involve herself in the curriculum to make sure that 'boy-friendly' subjects are taught, to have 'regular conferences' with her son's teacher and 'encourage' the school to employ more male teachers (2008, 166, 167, 169). Her phraseology suggests that these actions will be welcomed by teacher and school, and to be successful, exemplifying sociologist Anette Lareau's observation that middle-class parents not only expect schools to 'accommodate to their child's individualized needs' but also feel it is their right to voice those expectations (2008, 117). This attitude stands in stark contrast to the experiences of African American author Deborah Watkins. When she tries to ensure that her son receives fair treatment in school, she meets with very strong opposition, including rudeness from the child's teacher (2017, 109).

The advice books that can be attributed to Black authors address race explicitly throughout the text and some of them also signal it in the titles, as in *7 Principles for Raising Black Sons: A Practical Hand-Guide for Today's Single Black Mothers* (Estelle 2013) and *Single Mother's Guide to Raising Black Boys* (Lewis 2010). Walton and Caliendo observe that race is constructed both in 'cultural and political terms' (2021, 10), and this is very much the case in the advice books by African American authors. In addition to references to institutionalized racism in the educational and legal system, a number of the authors also discuss what is represented as a particular African American culture and community, both in positive and negative terms. Nancy Boyd-Franklin and A. J. Franklin, for example, stress the importance of 'building a strong racial identity' (2001, 2) and Patrick Phillips includes a chapter on the importance of making the sons take pride in their African American culture (2018,

127–133). Watkins notes how African Americans dominate in every field they decide to enter, be it sports, music or science (2017, 79). On the other hand, she discusses African Americans as particularly materialistic (2017, 35). Mervin Bourne Jr claims that African American culture makes men take great pride in impregnating as many girls as possible (2016, xiii), what Patricia Hill Collins refers to as 'myths of Black male hypersexuality' (2009, 189). A great many of the authors thus make references to 'us' African Americans, as sharing a stable, fixed, Black identity, regardless of, for example, class. In this, the authors can be said to be 'doing' both race and ethnicity in the way Moya and Markus discuss (2010). They construct race and ethnicity as a 'doing' rather than a being, where doing race includes 'sort[ing] people into ethnic groups' based on 'perceived … characteristics that are often imagined to be negative, innate, and shared' and doing ethnicity as identifying people 'with groupings' based on 'presumed, and usually claimed, commonalities' which may include 'physical appearance and/or ancestry group' (2010, 21–22). Using the term 'race', the advice authors group themselves and other African Americans together, based on a number of characteristics, both self-selected, positive ones, such as excelling at sports and showing community spirit, and ones imposed from the outside, often negative, such as laziness, lack of intellectual curiosity and sexual incontinence.

Class

Talking about class in reference to the United States is complicated, since it is often seen as a classless society, or, rather, most Americans refer to themselves as middle class (Kingston 2000, xv, 2). This has led to, it has been claimed, a situation where there is no shared language in the United States for discussions of class, which 'can leave us literally speechless on the topic' (Williams 2020, 11). This is evidenced in Lois Weis' study of the White working class, where she gives examples of how informants react to and reflect on class-based inequalities in their community by recasting them as problems of gender and race (2008, 295). Similarly, Paul W. Kingston argues that it is often used in 'popular "class analysis"' to account for 'economic *inequalities* in our society' (2000, 2, original emphasis). However, in her study of middle-class identities, sociologist Fiona Devine points out that this does not mean that Americans do not have a *concept* of class (2005). In fact, the informants she has interviewed use the 'language of class' as well as 'class labels', when constructing their identities as middle class (2005, 141). Class, albeit undefined, is thus part of US society.

How to define class, however, and in particular the very broad middle class, is thus potentially problematic. Different commentators, working within different disciplines, use different sets of criteria. The most basic criterion is income. If a person's income falls within a certain range, he or she is middle class. Below that, the person is working class, low-income or poor. Above that range, the person is upper class.

Adding more criteria allows for a more complex description. Anette Lareau, in her study of Black and White middle-class parents' transference of privilege to their children, includes 'occupational autonomy, usually in a professional or managerial position' as well as 'a college degree' (2008, 120). Kris Marsh and colleagues, analysing what they term the emerging Black middle class, rely on four factors: education, wealth (in the form of homeownership), income and occupation (Marsh et al. 2007, 741). In their assessment, middle class entails four years or more of college, owning one's own home, an income over the national median and a high-status occupation, such as, for example, physician, dentist, lawyer, teacher, government official (2007, 756). However, this definition of middle-class professions, based on OCCSCORE, an occupation score index, does not necessarily tally with people's perceptions. According to Joan C. Williams, professions such as lawyer, doctor and banker are not regarded as middle class by working-class people, but as belonging to the rich (2020, 9). Williams places such jobs in the 'professional-managerial class' which comprises 16.65 per cent of American households (2020, 10). The rather rigid structure used by Marsh et al. is very useful for statistics and for analysing demographic trends. However, it is less applicable in other contexts, such as that of the advice books. As Williams notes, class is about more than income; it is also 'a cultural tradition' people refer to when they 'shape their everyday behaviour and make sense of their lives' (2020, 12).

An approach closer to cultural traditions is used by Beverley Skeggs, who, in *Class, Self, Culture*, moves away from 'classificatory systems', from 'measuring classes to see how people fit into classificatory systems', to focus more on the 'how and why' of classifications (2004, 4–5). According to Skeggs, class is not fixed, but dynamically produced, so that, for example, 'the middle-class does not exist in ready-made reality' but is constantly re-created (2004, 5). Yet, the middle class is often referenced as if it is a fixed category, even by Skeggs herself. In her seminal study of the identity work of a group of British working-class women, *Formations of Class and Gender* (1997), she points to the difficulties of establishing exactly what the working class is but makes references to the British middle class as if there is a settled consensus. This is repeated by, for example, Sharon Hays. In her important work *The Cultural Contradictions of Motherhood* (1996), she references middle-class mothers and their expectations, without any delineations. Anette Lareau, however, gives an indication of what she means by the term in her book *Unequal Childhoods*, by juxtaposing parenting habits and expectations of middle- and working-class parents.

Similarly more specific is Elizabeth Currid-Halkett's analysis of what she has dubbed the 'aspirational class' (2018). In her study, she analyses specific habits, traditions and choices of what she views as a new elite. Although devoting a fair amount of space to discussions concerning aspirational people who are also rich, she makes the claim that the members of this class base their identity to a greater extent on knowledge 'irrespective of their economic means', so that what counts is, for example, 'being up-to-date on the news' and 'eating organic food' (2018, 18), rather than driving expensive cars and wearing designer clothes. She uses hipsters as an example, who, since they do not have much money, instead use their knowledge 'about what is cool or in the know', such as 'obscure blogs' or 'NPR canvas bags' to establish their position in this new elite (2018, 58).

Currid-Halkett's observations are particularly useful in connection with the motherhood practices of the aspirational class. What she describes is in some respects very similar to the practices of 'intensive mothering' that Hays investigated, where mothers are expected to devote 'a tremendous amount of time, energy, and money' to their childrearing (1996, x). The difference, however, is that the motherhood practices of the aspirational class are less about money (although that is important too) and more about 'extensive research into the perfect way to feed, console, and educate the under-three set' (2018, 20). The way some of these motherhood practices and expectations cut across class, race and income is exemplified by the way both Bay Buchanan – White, well-connected upper-middle class – and Deborah Watkins – Black middle class – place great value on music lessons for their children. Thus, for the purposes of this analysis, I will use an amalgam of the various definitions of middle class, including education, homeownership, income and profession. But I will also include ideas expressed concerning, for example, childrearing, expectations regarding access to and purposes of children's education as well as notions of morality and respectability.

In their analysis of factors obstructing the development of a Black bourgeoisie, William Darity et al. point out that 'the concept of the middle class and all its associated characteristics is a White-centered narrative' (2021, 501), and it should be noted that 'the black middle class experience differs from that of the white middle class' (Marsh et al. 2007, 741). However, as will be demonstrated, a number of the White characteristics are also embraced by Black middle-class authors, and they exhort their readers to emulate their own examples. Most of the authors of the advice books appear to fall into the category of middle class as defined by income, education, profession and housing. Almost all of them list some form of academic credentials and appear to have incomes above the cut-off point between working and middle class. Likewise, their jobs as doctors, therapists, social workers or various kinds of business entrepreneurs fall within the middle-class range. A few specifically reference homeownership, but since two-thirds of Americans own their own homes (Williams 2020), it seems safe to assume that most of the other authors do too. Many of them also subscribe to supposed middle-class ideas of childrearing, what Lareau terms 'concerted cultivation' (2011).

The mother readers interpellated by the White authors are middle class, as will be discussed, whereas the class of the readership of the Black authors is less clear. Some authors appear to address members of the working class, as defined by Williams. In her definition, working class designates those who earn less than the median income, do not have a college education and who have jobs such as, for instance, construction workers, physicians' assistants, health aides, sewage workers, paramedics and train drivers (2020, 5, 15). Other advice authors appear to address what is sometimes referred to as 'the working poor' (Labor 2016) – people who may work several jobs and still find it difficult to make ends meet. The topics covered by those authors also seem to include those discussed by Skeggs in her analysis of the British working class: morality, hygiene, respectability (1997).

Single Mothers: Class, Race and Stereotypes

Class figures prominently in public perceptions of single mothers in the United States. These days they are generally assumed to be working class and/or poor, but the public attitude towards single mothers has shifted in the United States during the twentieth century. In her study of the representation of poor women in US society after World War II, *From Good Ma to Welfare Queen*, Gender Studies scholar Vivyan Adair notes how single mothers have gone from being seen as deserving, respectable widows to scroungers, living off welfare (2000). These 'welfare women', outside patriarchal control, become 'a threat to the male subject and his society', connected to 'pathology', to 'sexual instability, disorder, and immorality' (Adair 2000, 14, xvi).

As Adair observes in regard to single mothers, when attitudes shift, class becomes closely enmeshed with race, so that '[w]idowed women with social security and divorced women with child support and alimony' are interpreted as White women, who stay in their homes, 'impart[ing] traditional cultural mores to their offspring' (Adair 2000, xvi). The single mother on welfare, who is assumed to be Black, 'is both the product and producer of a culture of disease and disorder' (2000, xvi). Professor of Political Science Ange-Marie Hancock makes the same observation in her book *The Politics of Disgust: The Public Identity of the Welfare Queen*, how the image of the recipient of welfare has gone from 'White Protestant widows and southern European immigrant mothers' to Black women (2004, 12).

In addition to class prejudice, African American single mothers are also subjected to the 'pathologizing discourse' of the 'poor mothering skills of Black women' (Hancock 2004, 26, 41). African American women in general, and mothers in particular, are often reduced to a few stereotypical characteristics, including unfeminine assertiveness, laziness and hyperfertility, what Patricia Hill Collins sums up as the 'controlling images' of 'matriarchs, welfare recipients and hot mommas' (2009, 76). These stereotypes were given widespread circulation in the United States through Daniel Patrick Moynihan's government report *The Negro Family: The Cause for National Action*, which was published in 1965. Compiled during the Civil Rights Movement, the intention was to avert a 'crisis in race relations' (1967, 43). What Moynihan saw as one of the major causes of this crisis was 'the deterioration of the Negro family' (1967, 51). In fact, the report was read by many to suggest that 'family pathology was more important than economic oppression' and other forms of systemic discrimination, which allowed some critics to claim that 'poor blacks were themselves to blame for their situation' (Jenkins 2007, 66).

The ultimate cause of this deterioration, Moynihan suggested, was the 'three centuries of exploitation' through slavery, but the proximate cause, and what needed to be fixed, was the 'family pathology' of the 'female family head' where fathers were 'no longer the provider' (1967, 51, 65). Tracing what he called the 'tangle of pathology' (1967, 76), he maintained that African Americans had been 'forced into a matriarchal structure' which placed 'a crushing burden on the Negro male' (1967, 75). The image of the Black single mother as the woman who is 'too strong' (Hancock 2004, 58), who is a 'castrating matriarch' (Adair 2000, xvi), has been reiterated ever since and she is often castigated for making it impossible for Black fathers to take up 'their rightful positions as head of the household' (Hancock 2004, 58).

This stereotype of African American women as not submissive enough is not restricted to White critics – as Collins notes, many Black men have 'accep[ted] the matriarchy thesis' (2009, 96), and it has often been claimed that 'Black men must ... regain their lost manhood' (2009, 170), so that they, as Candice Jenkins writes in *Private Lives, Proper Relations: Regulating Black Intimacy*, may take up their 'rightful place ... as the leader of the black family unit, in a dominant position vis-à-vis black women and children' (2007, 66). In this struggle, it is the task of African American women 'to unite the Black community [and] forego their own liberation' (Collins 2009, 94). As Collins points out, there is a difference between matrifocality and matriarchy: 'Black women's centrality in Black family networks should not be confused with matriarchal or female-dominated family units' (2009, 58). Yet, as will be demonstrated, the image of the too-strong African American woman who drives away partners and emasculates sons is widely referenced in the advice books.

The laziness of the African American woman is another long-standing stereotype, harking back to antebellum times (Hancock 2004, 6). In her guise as the welfare queen, the Black single mother is presented as 'content to sit around and collect welfare, shunning work and passing on her bad values to her offspring' (Collins 2009, 87). The African American single mother 'drains resources, doesn't work' and abuses the welfare system (Hancock 2004, 64). She would rather be on welfare than work to support herself and her children. Although the identity of the welfare queen is attributed to all single mothers, it is particularly resonant in discussions of Black single mothers. The supposed laziness and aggression are then combined into a paradoxical stereotype of the African American (single) mother who on the one hand spoils her son with too much lenience and on the other abuses him physically and mentally (King and Mitchell 1995, 9). Again, this is evidenced in the advice books, which accuse their mother readers of shouting at, belittling and hitting their sons, whilst simultaneously spoiling them to the extent that they are incapable of functioning as adults.

A further stereotype is that of the Black woman as hypersexual and hyperfertile (Hancock 2004, 6), often called the 'Jezebel' (Collins 2009, 89; Hancock 2004, 26; Jenkins 2007, 10). Black women in general have been represented as 'sexually aggressive' (Collins 2009, 89), and this links up with the welfare queen, who is 'unable to refuse the carnal pleasure that leads to pregnancy' (Jenkins 2007, 11). Since they are bad mothers, Black women will also transfer this sexual aggression and pleasure-seeking to their daughters, who are 'constructed as hypersexual and hyperreproductive' (Elliott, Powell, and Brenton 2015, 355). Collins sees these 'controlling images' as having not only to do with historical attempts to justify White sexual assaults on Black women but also a historical concern with regulating sexual production. Outside of producing new slaves, reproduction should be carried out by White middle-class women. Today these stereotypes and attempts at controlling fertility come into effect, not only in the media exploitation of African American female bodies (Littlefield 2008) but also in the way that African American young women are more likely to be prescribed more invasive and dangerous forms of contraceptives than White young women (Collins 2009, 94).

It should be noted, however, that although there are race-specific aspects to the stereotypes applied to Black single mothers, they are also linked to class. A number of the negative characteristics discussed by Collins, Hancock and others are also attributed to White working-class women. The 'White Trash Mama', to use Dawn Marie McIntosh's term, is also hypersexual, hyperfertile, relying on welfare, lacking in maternal skills and interest and aggressive towards men (2018, 105). The difference is that there are positive stereotypes of White motherhood, McIntosh's middle-class 'Supermom' for example (2018, 102), whereas there does not seem to exist a corresponding positive Black stereotype. As Collins notes in her analysis of the various controlling images Black women are subjected to, even those that seem at first glance to be positive, such as the 'Black lady', the 'middle-class professional Black woman', turn out to have negative repercussions (2009, 80). The Black lady, Collins argues, is a modernized version of the Mammy, someone 'who works twice as hard as anyone else' (2009, 81). She may not be subjected to criticism, but she is expected to sacrifice herself for the well-being of others.

Author Positioning

As noted in the introductory chapter, the advice book authors come from a variety of different social, political and educational backgrounds, and they present themselves and their credentials for giving advice in different ways. However, for those authors who are themselves single parents, this position is a particular challenge, considering the stigma that is still attached to single motherhood. On the one hand, a single mother who has successfully raised her son(s) to adulthood is in a position to give expert advice. On the other hand, there are the notions of pathology, lax morality and wilful dependence.

The White middle-class authors who are, or have been, single mothers all describe themselves as single mothers against their will, having been abandoned by their husbands (e.g., Buchanan 2012, x; Panettieri 2008, 9; Chisholm 2007, 32–33). Their children have all been born inside marriage and, in most cases, have memories of their fathers leaving the home. Most of the White authors are not single mothers, however, but happily married (e.g., Elium, Krause, Meeker) or male (e.g., Kennedy, Leman).

The African American, working-class or former working-class mothers, on the other hand, have almost exclusively given birth outside of wedlock. They are very careful, however, to stress that they had expected to marry the father (e.g., Jones 2015, 28; Pearson 2019, 2; Watkins 2017, 11) and that they are not to blame for their position as single mothers. Thus, although the circumstances of how they came to find themselves raising children on their own differ, all these women, Black and White, stress that they did not enter into this position willingly – these are not single mothers by choice.

The positions adopted by male authors are also worth considering. Some male authors, White or Black (e.g., Bromfield, Passley, Small), do not address whether they have children or not. Instead, their authority rests on their credentials as psychologists and therapists, or in the case of Small, as a successful businessman who has 40 years of experience helping 'families strengthen their relationships and improve their financial status' (Amazon author profile). Some Black or White male authors note that they are loving fathers in stable marriages (e.g., Bourne Jr, Leman). Some African American authors note that they do not have children, but that their community work or their status themselves as raised by single mothers enables them to give advice and guide others (e.g., Tardy).

Finally, there are a number of authors, mainly Black (e.g., Dennis, Franklin and Bryant) but also one White (Dickerson), who are themselves divorced fathers, or in the case of Bryant, never married, who do not live with their children. These non-custodial fathers choose different ways of connecting their life situations to their positions as authors. Dickerson merely writes that when he and his wife divorced, his boy 'became a son without a father. The fallout of divorce', but he makes no further comments (2012, 13). The African American male authors, however, have to contend with the spectre of the 'deadbeat dad', the (usually) African American father who takes no responsibility for his children. Thus these authors make a point of their devotion to their children. A. J. Franklin describes his family life as that of a 'blended family' in which he and his second wife co-parent the children from his first marriage together with his ex-wife (2001, 1). Dennis explains that it was his deployment in Afghanistan that ended his first marriage and emphasizes that he has tried to stay in touch with his sons (2015, 7). Bryant, who never married or lived with his son's mother, particularly lays himself open to criticism. However, he stresses his involvement with the boy and suggests that he has found some kind of 'middle ground'; although he has not married the mother, he 'remain[s] active in the child's life both developmentally and financially' (2015, 19). Yet, something these non-custodial fathers have in common is their generally unapologetic stance towards their absence. They tend to restrict themselves to a simple statement that they do not live with the children but love them and stay involved in their lives, even if it is only for a few weeks each summer (Dennis 2015, 8). This is very different from the extended explanations and the guilt expressed by the single mothers in connection with their status as single mothers.

Class and Race in the Advice Books

Class and race align in almost all the advice books analysed here. All the White authors write from a middle-class perspective, for a middle-class readership, but without acknowledging it. As will be shown, they make references to what they see as 'normal life' but which working-class people would regard as what Williams refers to as 'the display of class privilege' (2020, 31) The African American authors generally write for a working-class or low-income readership, and most of them have a working-class background, although they stress that through diligent studies and hard work they have become successful both socially and financially. A number of these books have a marked aspirational quality to them. The authors present themselves as successful entrepreneurs (e.g., Phillips, Anderson, Howland) and business people (e.g., Pearson, Dennis), and they specifically stress the importance of education as a means of achieving goals.

Class affects mothers' expectations of their children, as Sharon Hays has noted. As part of the research for *The Cultural Contradiction of Motherhood* (1996), she interviewed a large number of working-, middle- and upper-middle-class women.[1] In the book, she notes how attitudes concerning childrearing tend to cluster according to class, so that although all mothers want their children to do well, working-class and poor mothers emphasize the importance of 'formal education' where middle-class mothers are more concerned with their children's 'self-esteem' (1996, 86). Similarly, working-class mothers expect 'obedience' from their children and expect them to follow 'rules' (1996, 86). Middle-class mothers, on the other hand, are more likely to provide their children with 'choices' and 'negotiate' with them over those choices (1996, 86). Anette Lareau, in her study of Black and White working-class and middle-class children *Unequal Childhoods*, notes the same tendencies (2011). Middle-class parents aim for 'concerted cultivation'; whereas, working-class and poor parents strive for 'natural growth' (2011, 3). These patterns are repeated, to a great extent, in the advice books.

Books for a middle-class, White readership, for example, are to a greater extent concerned with the boy's mental and physical health, stressing the importance of preventing or combating alcohol and drug abuse, depression and suicide, presenting therapy as a given for any boy whose parents have separated (e.g., Allen and Dickerson 2012, 49; Chisholm 2007, 56). One book even labels growing up without a father as a 'syndrome' (Allen and Dickerson 2012, 10). Overall, middle-class White authors tend to focus more on biology, neuroparenting, health and borderwork grounded in medical research. The general focus of the Black authors is more on morality, on making sure boys show respect towards adults in general and women in particular, remain sexually continent and become good citizens. These concerns are exemplified by Khaz Estelle's wish to help mothers raise 'productive men of integrity and honor' (2013, 1) and Bourne Jr's complaint that African American young men measure their self-worth in the 'number of women they reproduce with' (2016, xiii). On the rare occasions when the Black authors address health (e.g., King 2015; Bryant 2015), it is often a question of personal hygiene. This may be a reflection of working-class concerns with hygiene as a signifier of respectability (Skeggs 2004, 4).

Education

In the United States, education has increasingly come to be seen as a requirement for any kind of success. As Currid-Halkett writes, 'today, a college education quite literally defines and predicts one's future income, occupation and class' (2018, 70). Middle-class parents expect their children to receive a good education as a matter of course (Lareau 2008) and this is evidenced in the middle-class advice books as well. Good education is presented as a given and after school, there is college, paid for by the parents (Meeker 2015, 153). It is taken for granted that the boys will attend good schools since '[e]ducational success' is important, not only because it brings financial stability but also because it brings 'personal satisfaction' (Bromfield and Erwin 2001, 221). As noted by, for example, Hays (1996) and Williams (2020), self-esteem and self-actualization are at the core of what middle-class parents want for their children.

Even though a good education is presented as something that routinely will be afforded the boys, the books highlight potential threats that the mother reader must be aware of. One of those is the anti-studying culture amongst boys (e.g., Bromfield and Erwin 2001, 224). Another, as was noted in the previous chapter, is the feminization of schools. A few authors also mention teachers' expectations that boys growing up without fathers will perform less well (Panettieri 2008, 3). It thus falls on the mother to ensure that the son receives as good an education as possible. As Lareau has noted amongst both Black and White middle-class parents, there is an assumption that 'they are entitled to have the institution accommodate to their child's individualized needs' and that if their demands are not met at the immediate level, they can escalate the matter higher up in the hierarchy (2008, 117). This is reflected in the books by White middle-class authors. It is taken as read that a mother can simply demand from her son's teacher that his needs are accommodated, and if this does not happen, she should turn to the principal. This is evidenced by, for example, Panettieri, Bromfield and Erwin and Buchanan. Allen and Dickerson suggest that the mother reader should ask the principal to employ more male teachers, or at least make sure that extant male teachers are assigned to boys without fathers (2012, 74).

Black authors, writing for a working-class readership, represent education and learning as a goal everyone knows must be fought for. They are well aware of how the school system is stacked against African American children, in particular boys (e.g., King 2015, 22). Black mother readers are told that they must be prepared to fight for their boys, not just against boys' supposed innate gendered disinclination to study, as well as the peer culture against schoolwork, but also against teachers, principals and school boards who have decided that poor Black boys cannot possibly do well in school. Watkins (2017), for example, describes her continual struggle to ensure that her sons obtain scholarships to get them into good, private schools, but also the struggle of making sure that they stay there, even though individual teachers, as well as the system, work against them. Howland relates a similar experience, where her son was discriminated against and expelled on what she considered to be very flimsy grounds (2020). Howland stands out, however, as the only African American author who expected the school to accommodate her son. Watkins, on the other hand, does not enter into the situation expecting to be accommodated without a fight.

The goals of education differ between books for middle-class and working-class readers. The books by middle-class authors tend to represent studies as a means to get into college. A number of Black authors, on the other hand, stress the importance of young Black men finding 'their passion' (Andersson 2017, 7–12) and their mothers creating '"opportunities for greatness"' (Bourne Jr 2016, 43). White boys are not exhorted to the same extent to find what inspires them. As noted in Hays' study of middle-class mothers, these mother readers are encouraged to make sure that the boys play sports and learn to play musical instruments and take part in 'the right outings' (1996, 63).

Several Black authors stress that the mother reader must help her son to find what it is that will ignite him, make him soar, make him exert himself. This could be interpreted as a reaction against cultural assumptions that Black men are lazy and not academically gifted, not interested in intellectual endeavours. Such an interpretation is supported by, for example, Watkins' question: 'Why does being curious about life translate to being white?' (73). In her book, she stresses repeatedly the importance of making sure that the children are 'exposed' – given access to learning, through museums, zoos and other institutions (Watkins 2017, 67) and laments the fact that many other African American mothers will not make the effort for their children. What she describes is a culture of not being interested, which she defines as a racial characteristic. However, it could also be argued that the different focus is a class issue (Lareau 2011, 5).

A few of the authors also discuss education for the mother readers themselves. White author Dana Chisholm describes how she went to night school several nights a week in order to finish her degree (2007, 80–81) and Black author Cederick Tardy urges the mother reader to '[c]ontinue your education past a high school level' and preferably also get a college degree (2006, 78). Both of them present education as a way of increasing one's earnings. However, a college degree does not necessarily pay off for Black students, as a study by the Center for Economic and Policy Research has showed (Jones and Schmitt 2014). Black graduates find themselves in unemployment, or 'underemployed', that is, in jobs that do not require a four-year college degree to a greater extent than students in general (2014, 1). The Black students are then left with paying off a student loan on a lower salary. Furthermore, higher education can actually count against Black graduates. Tomaskovic et al. found in a study of early career earnings trajectories of White, Hispanic and Black students that for Hispanics and Blacks the 'disadvantage in early career earnings is severest for those with the highest levels of education' (2005, 82). The conclusion drawn by Tomaskovic et al is that Blacks and Hispanics are paid less than Whites even when they have adequate education since their human capital 'is devalued in the labor market' and the effect 'increases with education' (2005, 83). In short, education is not necessarily the key to social mobility and wealth that the advice authors present it as; yet, of all the authors, White and Black, there are only two who suggest alternatives. King, for example, states that 'college is not for everyone' (2015, 23) and Philips argues for other forms of personal development, for example, through trade schools, 'pursuing entrepreneurship or the intentional use of military service' (2018, 118).

Personal finances

Single mothers are likely to have to struggle financially, which is a fact referenced by many of the advice book authors (e.g., Meeker 2015, xviii). However, authors addressing a working-class readership are more likely to address actual hardships, such as managing 'five jobs simultaneously' (Bourne Jr 2016, xvii). Overall, money is more of a topic in the books by African American authors, both the lack thereof and the way it is distributed – what the mothers might spend it on and whether they teach their sons how to earn it and spend it wisely. Some Black authors also give advice about organizations that might help fund summer camps, where to find free activities (Bourne Jr 2016, 45–46), and even how to save on electricity and buy food cheaply (Palmer 2013, 19, 23).

A few African American authors deviate from this pattern, however. Watkins, Pearson, Moffitt and Bolds reference a different background. Unlike the other authors, they grew up with both their biological parents, and Pearson references her grandfather's position as a pastor. Moffett mentions her parents' strong marriage and the fact that her father was a good provider. Bolds writes that her parents dedicated their lives to her. Watkins had a steady government job with health benefits and had bought her own house before she became a single mother. Although not all boxes of a middle-class position are necessarily ticked, the advice these authors give does resonate with middle-class ideals and expectations. As noted earlier, homeownership is important as a marker of wealth and something most Americans strive towards (Darity Jr, Addo and Smith 2020, Marsh et al. 2007). This attitude is shared by Watkins, who reiterates a number of times the importance of making sure that one at least has a home – privilege rent payments over everything else, and buy a house, but make sure it is in a good neighbourhood. There is no acknowledgement of the fact that the mother reader may not be able to be so circumspect if she has the means to buy a house at all.

Although White middle-class authors also acknowledge the fact that money might be tight, particularly after a divorce (e.g., Bromfield and Erwin 2001, xiii), they still presuppose a relatively affluent existence. Jamie Tyler simply advises the single mother to '**Be financially independent**' so that she is not a 'liability upon anyone' (2014, Chapter 1, original bold).[2] It is assumed that the single mother will be living with her children in a house (Panettieri 2008, 11; Chisholm 2007, 30), where one of the 'basics of life' is to have 'the carpets cleaned' (Chisholm 2007, 17). The mother reader is also expected to have a car[3] and be able to afford expensive sports and hobbies (Bromfield and Erwin 2001, 2; Panettieri 2008, 10; Adams 2011, 25). She is further assumed to be able to rearrange her working schedule so that she can watch the child's matches, even when they include weekend-long away games (Chisholm 2007, 87; Meeker 2015, 153). Buchanan even urges the mother reader to find a job that allows her to earn enough money, whilst working less, so that she can spend more time with the child (Buchanan 2012, 50). The mother reader is further given advice on suitable activities to bond with her son over, such as road trips and camping trips.[4] Again, the assumption is that she has the time and money to do this. As Hays notes, the activities the intensive mother is expected to carry out require 'a bottomless pocketbook' (1996, 63), and this seems to be reflected in the middle-class advice books.

Legal matters

Several of the advice books mention contact with the police and various legal matters. As noted earlier, a great many of the books have a list at the beginning of all the evils that may befall the boy who grows up in a fatherless home (e.g., Bromfield and Erwin 2001, xi). Included in this list is incarceration. Authors state that out of the many young men who are serving time in prison, a large percentage are men who grew up without a father in the home (Passley 2006; Dennis 2015). In a few cases, prison is given as one reason why fathers may be absent (e.g., Allen and Dickerson 2012, 9; Passley 2006, 20; Chisholm 2007, 24). However, the way the author refers to police involvement throughout the rest of the book varies greatly between books aimed at White or Black mother readers.

White authors refer to police officer as a profession young men might want to take up (Meeker 2015, 62; Engber and Klungness 2006, 279). Panettieri relates an instructive but engaging tale of how boys, unlike girls, will take risks, in which police officers feature as benevolent guardian angels (2008, 17). The White author who refers to the police the most is Buchanan, but this is again done in humorous anecdotes. These include how her brothers' weekend fighting in her youth repeatedly involved the police, how she was asked by the police to come and get two of her sons' friends from the holding cell after they were caught fighting during spring break and how her sons' reckless driving landed them in court 'a half-dozen times' (2012, 156, 119, 126). These stories are told to show the importance for a man of being able to hold his own in a fight, show her sons' high spirits and adventurousness and show her as a caring and supportive mother. In the world she describes, brushes with the law are merely that, amusing stories of young men being a bit boisterous, but with no long-lasting effects.

This stands in stark contrast to books by Black authors. In these narratives, brushes with the law can ruin a young man's life. Bourne Jr makes it clear that it is only the mother's firm hand that will keep her son out of prison (2016, 24). Bolds warns that not setting boundaries may lead to a phone call from the police, informing the mother reader that her son is now in jail (2008, 166). Watkins gives an extended example of how easily African American youths may be caught by the law, detailing how one of her sons was suspended from school, almost lost his scholarship, was taken to court, threatened with a year's imprisonment and finally put on probation for six months, simply for being present when a fight broke out during a football game (Watkins 2017, 142–145). Despite witnesses testifying that the young man had not been involved, he was faced with very serious consequences. Unlike Buchanan's sons, who although they had to 'explain their driving habits to judges' several times, seemingly suffered no ill effects (Buchanan 2012, 216), Watkins' son very nearly lost his place at school and almost went to prison, simply for being in the wrong place at the wrong time (142).

Several of the African American authors include chapters on the importance of teaching African American boys how to behave around police officers, in order not to be arrested or shot (e.g., Bryant 2015; Howland 2020; King 2015). Norwood has a chapter that includes a glossary explaining legal terms such as delinquent act, juvenile court and designated felony act (2016). This reflects the very different realities that White and Black authors are writing in, highlighting the White privilege. For a White mother reader, the boy may want to dress up as a police officer, and he may consider taking up the profession. For a Black mother reader, the police officer is a threat to her son, as is the rest of the legal system.

Religion

Since religion in one form or another is a prominent aspect of US society, it is also referenced in most of the advice books, to varying degrees. Some authors, such as Tina Krause, Dana Chisholm and Neil Kennedy, write from a specifically Christian perspective and give references to Bible passages. Other White authors, such as Allen and Dickerson (2012, 134) and Meeker (2015, 84), limit references to religion to the assumption that all mothers will have access to a rabbi/minister/priest for support.[5] They tend to suggest that the mother enrols her son in various activities run by the church in order to give him access to playmates and strong male role models. Bromfield and Erwin state that religion, 'regardless of denomination or type', will help 'building a healthy family' (2001, 176). Buchanan advocates quite strongly for taking the children to church every Sunday, even though she also makes it clear that it was a struggle for her to keep three unruly children in check, and there is no evidence in her text that she or they found any comfort in the worship or the community. Overall, White authors, unless outspokenly Christian, take a rather instrumental approach to organized religion, presenting it as a tool for keeping boys in check and transferring social codes.

The same diversity of religious expression is evidenced in the books by African American authors. Estelle, for example, limits himself to statements such as that the mother reader should ask 'God or Allah' to give her 'the power of forgiveness' (2013, 6). Other authors, such as Bourne Jr (2016) and Jones (2015), make God a constant presence in the text. Some of the books are also framed by religion in that they have forewords by religious leaders or testimonials from editors or youth leaders referencing the authors' religious commitment (King 2010; Moffitt 2020; Moore and Moore 2013). Furthermore, most books by African American authors take it for granted that the mothers are going, or should be going, to church regularly, and exhort them to make sure that their sons go too. Overall, the support that can be had from a religious community is often referenced in the African American books. Watkins, for example, acquires legal aid for free from a lawyer who is part of her church (2017, 145).

Williams notes that religion is important to White working-class people because it 'provide[s] the kind of mental exercise, stability, hopefulness, future orientation, impulse control, and social safety net many in the professional elite get from their families, their career potential, their therapists, their bank accounts' (2020, 21). These are some of the things also brought up by Black authors when they encourage the mother reader to make sure that her son goes to church. The White middle-class authors, on the other hand, when referencing religion as more than a source of role models for the boy and someone who will take him camping, focus on a personal relationship with God. Again, the idea is of self-actualization rather than community.

Expectations Placed on Mothers

Through the articulation of support and advice given, the books discursively construct the ideal mother, by stating what is expected of her, what she must and must not do. It has been suggested that advice books on childrearing really have more to do with regulating mothers (Hardyment 2007). It has been a given in Western culture for centuries that mothers should be kind, patient, nurturing and, above all, self-sacrificing. One particularly poignant example is how Donald Winnicott's highly influential concept of 'good enough mothering' nevertheless requires the mother to take pleasure in every aspect of childrearing, including being soaked in the child's urine (Doane and Hodges 1993, 25). However, the self-sacrifice took on new forms towards the end of the twentieth century. As noted earlier, maternal self-sacrifice includes what Hays called 'intensive mothering' (1996, x). This ideology 'encourages mothers to limit their own pursuits in the interest of their children' (Elliott, Powell, and Brenton 2015, 366), and it is also a feature of the 'paranoid parenting' articulated by Frank Furedi (2008) and the fixation on 'the maximisation of individual achievement potential' which causes mothers to overload their children with extra tuition and extracurricular activities in a variety of fields (Faircloth, Hoffman, and Layne 2013, 4).

Further research has established how widespread and entrenched this ideology is in the West (for an overview, see Elliott, Powell, and Brenton 2015, 352) but also that it is prevalent in other parts of the world (Faircloth, Hoffman, and Layne 2013, 14). Intensive mothering is usually 'coded White and middle class' (Elliott, Powell, and Brenton 2015, 352), yet, most mothers, regardless of race and socioeconomic status, also feel a 'pressure to conform'. In their study of low-income, Black single mothers, Elliott et al. show how these mothers position themselves in relation to this ideology, in an effort to fulfil the criteria of good mothers. They found that the women they interviewed tended to repeat the same ideas and ideals as those articulated in studies of White mothers (2015, 355). In particular, the researchers noted that 'the women believe that good mothers sacrifice for their children' (2015, 356). Yet, a great deal of the intensive mothering done by African American single mothers is not recognized as such, they note, since it focuses on different arenas from those of White middle-class mothers. Rather than 'music lessons or private tutoring', these women try to protect their children from the results of 'poverty, racism, and sexism' (2015, 366). Yet, again, it should be noted this supposed racial difference also pertains to class, as Lareau found, with her observation of middle-class concerted cultivation and working-class natural growth (Lareau 2011). Still, the attitudes towards intensive mothering are reflected in the advice books, where both groups of authors use the discourse of sacrifice, but it takes on different meanings depending on the intended readership.

The White authors, in particular, stress that the child must come first; being a single mother means having to listen to the child rather than being on the phone to a friend, watching television or checking e-mails. It also means placing the child's emotions first. Swanson writes: 'Stop what you are doing and really listen to him' (2019, 21). Panettieri tells the mother reader to respond to a toddler's 'high-pitched scream' as quickly as possible, even though it might be inconvenient, since 'there's nothing more important you could possibly be doing than being with your own child' (2008, 154). Buchanan similarly stresses the notion of sacrifice: 'Sacrifice is the central theme in the lives of all good moms'; 'you have to sacrifice mightily'; 'for your kids' sake, you have to be willing to sacrifice' (4, 8, 9). For Buchanan, being a single mother means giving up any right to privacy, me-time, or interests beyond the children (e.g., 2012, 46, 48).

Another theme that is repeated is the neoliberal emphasis on the individual and on the availability of choice. The mother readers are often addressed as 'subjects who will make sense of their lives through discourses of freedom, responsibility and choice—no matter how constrained they may be (e.g. by poverty or racism)' (Ehrstein, Gill, and Littler 2020, 196). Responsibility is strongly pushed, for example, by Buchanan, suggesting that there is no excuse for a single mother to fail – not economic, emotional or social (2012, x). It is simply a question of 'reach[ing] deep inside yourself and find[ing] the strength, courage and tenacity' to succeed (2012, 177). This is also an opinion echoed by Black authors. Although some of them describe how valuable church communities are, the overall message is that success in raising a Black boy into a productive American citizen, of 'releasing Kings out into the world and not Killers' is achieved through individual effort, not through reliance on the government (Watkins 2017, 148).

Most of the authors, regardless of race or class, appear reluctant to see themselves or their readership as part of a system and are unwilling to view government policy on childcare, minimum wage or education as linked to the problems a single mother faces. Black author Denise Bolds is the only one to suggest that the lives of single mothers would be made easier if better 'maternity benefits, employer childcare locations and breastfeeding locations' were introduced (2008, 9). The general attitude is quite similar to Lee et al.'s observation that risk consciousness sees '"parenting" as the cause of, and solution to, social problems' (2014, 16); in short, the various problems single mothers and their sons may face are the result of the mothers' individual choices, and they can only be resolved by the mothers' own actions.

It is repeated in a number of the advice books, particularly the autobiographical ones, that change lies in the mother's own hands; she must put the hurt of abandonment behind her and create opportunities for herself and her son. Buchanan, for example, states that single mothers must draw on their 'infinite reservoir of strength' and should receive a 'greater appreciation' from society for their hard work (2012, xi). She does not envisage single mothers receiving any kind of tangible support, however. Chisholm presents the wife of President John Adams as a role model. During the Revolutionary War, she took care of their five children while he was away fighting for eight years. She did this 'with no child support, no government assistance' (2007, 26). This attitude is echoed by the Black single mothers interviewed by Eliot at al. who 'embraced and performed intensive mothering in the absence of larger social supports for their children's upbringing' (2015, 365). The Black advice authors chime in with the attitude that mothers can, and will have to, do it on their own, 'kick the excuses out the window' and get on with the work (King 2015, 6). Lewis, for example, equates welfare with 'slavery' (2010, 57). There does not seem to be any discernible pattern of difference based on the gender of the author. Rather, it appears that they are all trying to avoid the stigma of the welfare queen, constructing the mother reader as a strong individual who can succeed without recourse to government aid.

The books thus display a reluctance to view the mothers and their situations in a wider context and through the lens of intersectionality. Instead, the women are addressed as 'entrepreneurial and responsibilised' subjects (Ehrstein, Gill, and Littler 2020, 198), whose circumstances are presented as the results of their own choices and not linked to class and socioeconomic structures. Even when relating their own biographical experiences, the authors do not make 'connections between their own personal lives and the structural forces that shaped' them (Brannen and Nilsen 2005, 423). As Zygmunt Bauman argues, people view their lives from the point of individualization and do not look for the ways in which 'society as a whole operates' and affects them (2001, 9). Brannen and Nilsen note that the 'choice biography', suggesting that people have agency and a say in the way their lives develop, even when they do not, may comfort the subject that she is not 'seemingly at the mercy of forces beyond [her] control' (2005, 423). This is reflected in the books, where choices are both seen as bad decisions that have landed the mother reader into trouble, and the way out of it. Chisholm, for example, describes the poor choice she made, marrying a man she knew would be an unsuitable husband, and how it then becomes solely her choice and responsibility to raise her children alone. Pearson has a chapter titled 'THE

CHOICE IS YOURS' in which she states that the reader can do and be anything she wants (2019, 6). Palmer, rather glibly, tells the reader to '[m]ake the choice to be happy' (2013, 35).

Even racism is in some ways not seen as a systemic problem – Watkins, for example, who in other sections of her book discusses the effects of it, ridicules experts who blame the situation of African Americans on 'post-traumatic slave syndrome, conspiracies, and oppression' (2017, 67). Other authors also acknowledge that racism is a factor in the lives of African Americans while simultaneously arguing that the mothers must pull themselves up by their bootstraps. The mothers are encouraged to seek help from their community or their church, but they are not encouraged to seek or expect help from the government. As noted earlier, this might in part have to do with the stigma of the welfare queen. But there is also no discussion of minimum wage or other kinds of legislation that might make it easier for single mothers to acquire qualifications that would allow them to find higher paying jobs. Instead, it becomes the task of the mother alone, to find a high-paying job with flexible working hours (Buchanan) that allows her to buy her own home (Watkins) and spend as much time as possible with her children (Palmer). If she does not have the qualifications, she should attend community college or something similar, but again without any government assistance (Chisholm). At most, she should call on friends and relations for help, but take care not to ask for too much (Chisholm 2007; Watkins 2017).

Maternal sexuality

The fact that mothers may wish to have active sex lives has been problematic in Western culture for a very long time, and this is also reflected in US society and in the advice books analysed here. Contemporary US society can still be seen as reflecting the 'republican family ideal' of the nineteenth century and the 'cult of true womanhood' (Jenkins 2007, 7). Part of this ideal is the 'purity' of the mother, which includes no display of sexual desires. The tension between maternal purity and the recognition that mothers are women too is evidenced in the way the advice books address the question of mothers dating. Although all of the advice books stress the importance of male role models for the young boys, the mothers dating and possibly remarrying is presented as a potentially problematic issue.

Books aimed at White middle-class mothers tend to either advise caution and urge mothers not to introduce partners too early, or warn mothers against remarrying, since stepfathers may have a detrimental effect on the growing boys; men find it difficult to feel 'parental love towards children that are not related to them' (Allen and Dickerson 2012, 129). According to Bromfield and

Erwin, 'unrelated males liv[ing] in a household' increases the 'risk of sexual molestation or child abuse' (2001, 260). To these authors, mothers dating and remarrying can be outright harmful to the young boys, emotionally and physically. Overall, however, a mother dating is represented as fairly uneventful, if she makes a wise choice and takes it slowly (Panettieri 2008, 218). It is generally assumed that she is dating for keeps – she is looking for a new husband. As Tyler writes: 'It's not a fling that you are looking for. You want a full-fledged relationship' (2014, Chapter 6). The only author who advises against mothers dating at all is Buchanan, who writes that since a single mother's time not spent at work should be devoted solely to her children, there simply is no time for dating until the children have grown up and left home (2012, 58). In short, apart from Bromfield and Erwin, who caution against mothers having 'numerous sexual relationships' (171), maternal sexuality is not addressed by White authors. If mothers wish to remarry, it is assumed this is because they think their sons would benefit from a father figure. That mothers may have sexual needs is not acknowledged. Palmer is one of very few authors to encourage the mother reader to go on dates, but it is framed as a stimulating break from childcare, on a par with sky diving or having one's nails done (2013, 41). Bromfield and Erwin are perhaps the most outspoken, suggesting that the mother reader should not subject the child to 'in-your-face affection on the couch' which can be 'too stimulating, confusing, and destructive' for the child (2001, 263).

The tone in books aimed at Black mothers is harsher, more accusatory. In her book *Black Feminist Thought*, Patricia Hill Collins references interviews with African American women who feel that they only have two positions to choose between, 'asexual mothers' or 'hypersexual whores' (Collins 2009, 169). This limited range is echoed in a number of advice books by male African American authors. In these books, there are very few, if any, positive references to mothers dating. The readers are warned against choosing partners who will disrespect them in front of their children, and several authors reference either their own childhood experiences or anecdotal evidence of other single mothers' promiscuous sex life (e.g., Dennis 2015, 46; Anderson 2017, 30; King 2015, 11) as well as the violence unsuitable boyfriends will inflict on mother and child (Bourne Jr 2016, 23). Bolds warns that arguing with a partner in front of the son may 'quickly escalate into violence and even death' (2008, 192), although it is unclear who would kill whom. Some authors also refer to mothers allowing their daughters to have a series of unsuitable boyfriends, resonating with the claim of the hyperreproductivity of the daughters of Black single mothers (Littlefield 2008). Extrapolating from their own childhood experiences, these authors apply them to the lives of most African American single mothers, reiterating the stereotypes and controlling images discussed earlier.

In her study of changes to US fatherhood, Nancy Dowd highlights how African American family structures deviate from the perceived norm, that Black women are less likely than White to marry if they fall pregnant (2000, 67). This is shown in the life stories of some of the African American authors. Watkins and Pearson both became pregnant in relationships, but for various reasons did not marry the fathers of their children. Bryant was in a relationship where his girlfriend became pregnant, but they never lived together and as he relates it, he never considered marrying her (2015, xiii). Dowd further demonstrates how African American fathers, despite never living with their children, still parent successfully and actually have a higher degree of involvement with their children than White fathers (2000, 70). This is not acknowledged by the African American authors, however. Instead, they tend to reiterate stories of absent fathers, although many of them lay the blame for this on the single mothers (e.g., Bryant 2015). In his book, Dennis quotes a number of informants, both female and male, who criticize Black single mothers for thinking that they do not need a partner (2015, 27). It is assumed that there is a culture in the Black community of women deciding to raise children without a husband, resonating with the stereotype of the matriarch, the too-strong woman, who drives away all men (Hancock 2004, 58). So for some authors, mothers should not be allowed to go on dates, to remarry; for others, mothers should not be allowed to think that they can manage without a husband.

In the way the issues of dating and maternal sexuality are addressed in the advice books, contradictory ideologies come into play. One is that women should rely on husbands rather than government support; therefore, they should remarry. Another is that mothers are not sexual beings. They should put their children first at all times and are not allowed to express or live out sexual urges; therefore, they should not date and not seek to remarry.

Reader Address

The way the books address the intended mother reader reflects society's ambiguous relationship to single mothers. All the books take as their starting point that they want to help single mothers carry out the very difficult task of raising a boy to manhood; they want to 'empower' the mother (Dennis 14). Denise Bolds writes that she wants to 'uplift black single mothers' (2008, 7). Derrick Moore exclaims 'I know you can do it!' (Moore and Moore 2013, 16). Some African American authors also call the single mothers 'walking superheroes' (Phillips 2018, 12), the 'back bone' of society (Joyce 2018, 119; Anderson 2017, x) and similar epithets, which ties in with the 'mother glorification' evidenced in the writing of African American men (Collins 2009, 188).

This type of praise, relying on the image of the 'superstrong Black mother', actually requires that Black mothers place everybody else's needs, particularly her son's, before her own (2009, 188). This is less prevalent in books by White authors, who confine themselves to simple statements of support, such as when Bromfield and Erwin note that bringing up a boy as a single mother 'does not doom him to juvenile delinquency, unhealthy relationships, or a second-class life' (2001, 12).

The question of whether a woman can raise a boy to be a man is addressed by both Black and White authors. Pearson states repeatedly that society will tell the single mother that she is not up to the task, and says that this is wrong. Chisholm makes similar claims. Yet, as Bromfield and Erwin write, what the mother reader needs is 'not sugar-coated pabulum, but realism and honesty' (2001, xv). Realism and honesty is what all the books claim to offer, in the form of guilt trips, scaremongering and, in some cases, outright accusations of how the mother invariably makes her son physically ill (Allen and Dickerson 2012), emotionally crippled (Bourne Jr 2016) and unable to form relationships with either men or women (Dennis 2015), to name but a few.

In addition to the biological, essentialist failings of single mothers, the authors, both Black and White, construct the mother reader as a woman who is bitter and resentful, who might prevent her children from seeing their father, or who distresses her son with her 'depression and neediness', requiring the son to take over as 'father to the other siblings, disciplinarian and spokesperson for the family' (Allen and Dickerson 2012, 83), who treats her son as her counsellor (Dennis 2015, 6; Joyce 2018, 55; Panettieri 2008, 220) or expects the son to function as her soul mate (Bromfield and Erwin 2001, 209). A great many of the authors will state emphatically that the mother must not make her son 'the man of the house', suggesting that this is something most single mothers will do (e.g., Adams 2011, 173; Bromfield and Erwin 2001, 78; Chisholm 2007, 150; Engber and Klungness 2006, 281; Joyce 2018, 4; Meeker 2015, 300; Passley 2006, 80; Phillips 2018, 96).

In fact, all the books are rude and/or patronizing towards the mother reader at some point, but to different degrees. White authors, such as Meeker, make throwaway comments suggesting that the mother reader is likely to put her own emotions first: if the son opens up to his mother, she must not 'turn the focus on yourself' and ask 'how in the world does he think that makes you feel' (2015, 22). Bromfield and Erwin instruct the mother reader to pay attention to the child's homework, rather than giving it a 'yeah, great' in order to 'get back to your favorite show' (2001, 226). Buchanan tells the mother reader to do her duty no 'matter how busy or tired you are' (2012, 128). Allen and Dickerson assume that the mother reader will prioritize phone calls to friends over dealing with her child's problems (2012, 120). Swanson simply tells the reader to put the phone down and give the child her 'undivided attention' (2019, 21). Thus, the mother reader is told on the one hand that she is too soft on the child, as discussed in Chapter 2, but she is also assumed to be selfish and distracted, failing to note and meet her child's needs. In some cases, the books will give advice that seems rather self-evident, such as that the mother reader should play with the boy and respond to the baby's cries (e.g., Bromfield and Erwin 2001, 40). There are hints in the books by White authors of an assumption that mothers do not know what they are doing. Bromfield and Erwin even state explicitly that although they do not subscribe to the view that only a man can raise a boy, they 'disbelieve that women are mythological deities who can always do it better' (2001, xv). This claim that women, despite their alleged nurturing nature, actually have no greater authority as carers is also echoed by Allen and Dickerson. In short, these authors simultaneously support and undermine mothers.

However, claims of actual maternal incompetence are more prevalent in the writing of several of the Black authors. These references resonate with the stereotype of Black women as 'bad mothers who care more for themselves than their children' (Hancock 2004, 41). Dennis, Bourne Jr, Anderson and Watkins all make comments on mothers who spend what little money they have on clothes, hair extensions and manicures for themselves. Some authors further assume that mother readers 'take on a very aggressive, confrontational stance' with their sons, shouting at them, belittling them at the slightest provocation (Bourne 2016, 23, see also Passley 2006, 68–69; Pearson 2019, 23), which draws on the stereotype of the too-strong woman who oppresses the men around her. Simultaneously, the African American mother reader is criticized for spoiling her son, never 'tell[ing] him no', never asking him to 'clean up after himself' (Bourne 2016, 4), 'wait[ing] on [him] hand and foot' King 2015, 48). Regardless of whether the mother is too loving, or not loving enough, it is the single mothers' fault that an 'entire generation of young men are spoiled rotten' and fail to realize that their actions have consequences (Bourne 2016, 13, 18).

In addition to assuming that the mother reader is lazy, too aggressive and too soft, a number of the African American authors also assume that she lacks not only mothering skills but also an interest in her children, and basic knowledge about the world. Palmer tells the mother reader to 'play with your child. Don't just be in the same house' (2013, 15). Watkins, like many of the authors, both Black and White, gives the mother reader a number of tasks to perform. But hers assume that the African American mother reader does not know what her child likes and dislikes, asking her to reflect on what she has 'learn[ed] about your children's interests' (2017, 40). She references a number of instances of Black mothers who are simply not interested in expanding their children's horizons, because they 'didn't have the time' or it will be too expensive (2017, 73–74). Palmer gives advice on saving money which seems to assume a complete lack of understanding of how finances work (2013, 18).

In short, White authors construct the mother reader as thoughtless at times, but generally competent, as long as that competence is not related to anything that falls within the purview of fathers. Black authors, on the other hand, reiterate a number of the stereotypes of the Black mother, particularly the poor and single, as lazy, selfish, uninterested in her children and lacking in even basic mothering skills. This construction of the African American single mother might be construed as an effect of what Candice Jenkins refers to as the 'salvific wish' – a wish to protect Black communities from censure based on cultural stereotypes, 'through the embrace of conventional bourgeois propriety in the areas of sexuality or domesticity' (2007, 14). Jenkins argues that a 'female version' of this wish includes 'a call for self-control or self-denial' whereas the male version tends towards 'the disciplinary and externally corrective', which includes 'policing black female sexuality' (2007, 14, 29). I would argue that the salvific wish could explain some of the very strong condemnations that are evidenced in the books by African American authors.

On the surface, there is thus great diversity between the books when viewed from the position of race. However, when looking more closely, and bearing in mind studies of White working class, it becomes apparent that a number of the issues discussed are not quite as race-dependent as some of the African American authors make them out to be. And when taking a step back, it becomes clear that the overall message is the same – single motherhood is problematic and to be avoided, since women are not fit to raise boys to be men.

Chapter 4

REINSTATING THE FATHER: FATHERS IN ADVICE BOOKS FOR MOTHERS

In Chapter 2, I discussed the borderwork that some advice authors undertake, attempting to demonstrate which particular aspects of childrearing that only fathers carry out. Some authors also betray an anxiety that fathers will be completely excluded from their children's lives. William Small, for example, writes of his concern that media representations of single mothers give 'the impression that a daddy is not necessary' (2017, x). John Dennis notes that one of the most common phrases on television when a sportsman, or an actor or just a person in the street is interviewed is 'Hi mom' (2015, 17). Yet, fathers loom large even in their absence in these advice books. It is claimed that good male role models will suffice, but many of the authors still write to and about the missing father, making these books 'sites in which discourses on fathering are reconstructed and reproduced' (Hunter, Riggs, and Augoustinos 2020, 151). As Hunter et al. argue, it is important to 'consider the implications of such discourses' (2020, 151). Not only do they affect fathers and the way they approach caregiving, but they may also affect and shape the way mother readers care for their sons.

Beginning with a brief[1] overview of how societal attitudes towards fatherhood have changed over the last century, including how fathers have been represented in media and popular culture, I then move on to an analysis of how fathers are presented in the advice books, with a particular focus on the privileging of fathers over mothers. The chapter then concludes with a brief analysis of advice books aimed at (single) fathers raising daughters. I juxtapose them as regards type of advice given, reader address and parental sexuality. As will be evident, the most striking difference is the way the father reader is assured of his centrality in his daughter's life. Many of the books are read as an attempt to persuade the father to involve himself with her, which is quite different from the message given to the mothers.

Fathers in Times of Change

In historical and sociological investigations of fathers and fatherhood, there is an intriguing movement, where the figure of the authoritative father is shunted ever backwards. Ralph LaRossa, writing on US fatherhood of the 1920s and 1930s, notes that at the time of his writing, there is a 'belief that yesterday's fathers not only did not want to be involved with their children, but did not even give the subject much thought' (1997, 4). Research on men of the post-war period contrast them 'to a more traditional image of absent, authoritarian fathers' (Haywood and Mac and Ghaill 2003, 44). Historians studying the early twentieth century may place the traditional father in the late nineteenth century, but when scholars study the nineteenth century, the authoritarian father is moved to the colonial era (Johansen 2001, 4–5) or to Europe (Kimmel 2012, 38). The illusive authoritarian father is thus never found in the period in question; he is what the fathers studied position themselves against. At the same time, research shows there is a yearning amongst some men for a position of greater authority as fathers and breadwinners, particularly in the fatherhood responsibility movement that has developed since the 1990s (Gavanas 2004, 1).

The great socio-economic upheavals in the United States during the twentieth century, including World War I, the Depression, World War II and then the boom of the 1950s, the deteriorating economy from the 1960s onwards, the feminist movement and civil rights movement, affected family structures and undoubtedly had an impact on how fathers, mothers and childrearing were regarded and experienced.

In the 1920s and 1930s, the idea of the father as 'economic provider, pal and male role model', which had developed in earlier periods (Leverenz 2003, 25), became institutionalized (LaRossa 1997, 1). The father was particularly important in counteracting the supposedly pernicious influence of mothers on their children (Griswold 1993, 94). Surfacing in the 1920s, but becoming fully developed in the 1940s, was the fear of the damaging influence of the overly powerful mother, sometimes referred to as Momism. This idea, first articulated by Philip Wylie in his book *Generation of Vipers* (1942) and Edward Strecker in *Their Mother's Sons* (1947), raised the alarm that American mothers were ruining their sons, making them unfit for society in general and for war in particular (Plant 2010). Fathers thus played a very important role in the family, saving the sons from the emasculating effects of their mothers, and functioning as role models for their daughters, so that they would know what to look for in their future husbands (Griswold 1993, 97). In fact, fathers' involvement with their children became one of the defining features of 'middle-class respectability' after World War II

(1993, 187). The construction of masculinity and of fatherhood continued more or less along the same lines in the 1950s and 1960s. The breadwinner ideal remained a central notion (Gillis 2000, 231). The father was supposed to be the undisputed leader and centre of the household, although James Gilbert, in his study of masculinity in the 1950s, has pointed to feelings of '"male panic"', when life in the suburbs as well as mass culture was depicted as 'feminizing' (2005, 2, 4). Many men looked to a 'renewal of traditional masculine vigor' as a remedy (2005, 4).

However, the changing economy from the 1970s onwards, resulting in fewer jobs available, weakened the links between fatherhood and masculinity, leading to a perceived marginalization of fatherhood (Gillis 2000, 230, 234). It became more and more difficult to support a family on one income. Middle-class women joined the workforce, not only out of necessity but also out of choice. There was a growing feeling that men, particularly White men, were being cheated out of what was rightfully theirs (Kimmel 2013). Now they had to compete with women, people of colour and immigrants for jobs, and there was a growing feeling of uncertainty about the future.

In addition to this, divorce rates went up. Women were no longer content to stay in bad marriages, now that they had the economic means to leave and take the children with them. Many men felt stiffed, to borrow Susan Faludi's term. There were growing concerns amongst some men that they were being marginalized, that parenting was being feminized and that 'family' was coming to mean only 'mother and child' (Gavanas 2004, 33). These worries and concerns were some of the contributing factors to the fatherhood movement of the 1990s (Gavanas 2004).

As society changed, the representations of fathers in popular culture also changed. In the 1950s, the father figures tended to be absent or authoritarian (Armengol-Carrera 2008) or well-meaning, but bumbling and inept (Gilbert 2005; Hamamoto 1989). Beginning in the 1980s, fathers were increasingly shown as 'nurturant, caring, and emotionally attuned', as the 'androgynous' father (Furstenberg 1988, 193). Sitcoms now presented the 'new, enlightened, participatory dad' in, for example, *The Cosby Show* (Douglas and Michaels 2005, 106) or the 'sensitive, nurturing, postfeminist men' in, for instance, *Family Ties* (Dow 2006, 121). Yet, even though there may be a greater diversity of types of fathers in the twenty-first century, they are still often presented as inept and bumbling (Pehlke et al. 2009). These various constructions of fathers have developed into what Hannah Hamad has termed postfeminist fatherhood, which represents fathers as equally competent at parenting, if not more so (2014), suggesting a sense of competition between fathers and mothers. I have discussed elsewhere the way in which popular culture narratives predicate fatherly competence and involvement on the absence of mothers

(2017). Such narratives may also be interpreted as a response to maternal gatekeeping.

Although changing concepts of fathering, such as 'involved fatherhood', 'caring masculinity' and fathers as primary caregivers do form a part of the public discourse (Hunter, Riggs, and Augoustinos 2017, 2020) and many fathers express a desire to be more active as caregivers (Doucet 2016), pregnancy guidebooks, medical brochures and parenting magazines tend to present fathers as secondary caregivers, being mothers' helpers rather than parents in their own right (Fleming and Tobin 2005; Schmitz 2016; Sunderland 2006; Wall and Arnold 2007). This too can be read as a form of maternal gatekeeping, and these constructions may inform the way the advice books for single mothers address the concept of fathers.

In the preface to David Blankenhorn's 2007 *The Future of Marriage*, it is stated that Blankenhorn has spent his career 'restoring fatherhood to the prominence it deserves' (2007, xi). This neatly sums up the aim of the work of not only Blankenhorn, David Popenoe and other authors, but also more popular and populist writers such as Farrell and Gray, and award-winning journalists such as Paul Raeburn, who writes about 'the parent we've overlooked' (2014). They start from an idea that fathers have a different, biologically grounded way of parenting, different from mothers, and that they possess a 'uniqueness [that] is essential', in particular to ensure that the growing boy becomes 'a good man' (Dowd 2000, 9). In her book *Redefining Fatherhood*, Nancy Dowd describes two predominant patterns of fatherhood: 'men who are significantly involved in the nurture of their children' and the 'dominant mode of fatherhood which involves minimal or no caretaking, with no other connection or contribution to the children' (2000, 22). As will be shown, this 'dominant mode of fatherhood' is the one most prevalent in the advice books, even by male authors who present themselves as involved fathers.

Fathers in the Advice Books

The question of what a father contributes to a family is addressed in Anette Lareau's article 'My Wife Can Tell Me Who I Know' (2000). In her interviews with a large number of fathers, both residential and divorced, it became evident that a large proportion of the fathers, despite claiming to be intimately involved with their children, were rather ill-informed about the children's day-to-day lives, such as the names of their children's friends and how they felt about their hobbies (2000, 408). Still, in their observations, Lareau and her team found that the fathers constituted 'a powerful presence in the household', 'creating laughter, promoting athletic development and masculinity' and 'providing a "gravitational center" for conversation' (2000, 409).

This view of the centrality of fathers recurs throughout the advice literature. In the books, fathers do not, and are not expected to, deal with carework such as changing nappies, feeding or giving emotional comfort. Instead, when the authors list the important aspects of fathering, they focus on physical activities – rough-housing is mentioned by many of the authors – and providing fun. Several of the authors point specifically to how mothers tend to be boring parents, obsessing about mundane matters such as not getting clothes dirty. Hunter et al. in their study of parenting texts aimed at fathers as primary caregivers (such as stay-at-home fathers) describe this construction of fathers as 'lively, physical and playful compared to mothers' as using masculinity in order 'to engage fathers' (2020, 166). In the advice books for mothers, it functions as yet another form of borderwork, presenting physicality, play, inventiveness and adventure as unique, male skills.

Fathers are better parents than mothers are

To make the case that fathers are needed, some of the advice books take issue with the notion that women are particularly suited to childrearing. Dennis quotes an informant who makes the simple observation that '"*men raise children better than women*"' (original italics 2015, 73). Allen and Dickerson write that women have 'perpetuated the myth' that childrearing is 'their exclusive domain', a myth they attempt to dismantle (2012, 19). They argue, for instance, that empathy is central to a boy's maturation into a good adult, and this can only be taught to him by his father or a father substitute, partly because men are particularly good at empathy and partly because the 'most qualified teacher for a son is his dad' (2012, 40). What these and many other advice authors have in common is the need to articulate as a fact that not only do men have certain innate qualities as parents that women lack but that they, overall, are better parents. Other authors limit themselves to noting that fathers 'are critical to the healthy emotional, physical, and intellectual development of boys' (Meeker 2015, 4).

One area in which fathers are superior is in their ability to be consistent in their parenting. Unlike mothers, who will be swayed by their softer emotions, fathers will make a rule and stick to it. Mothers might want to be friends with their children, but fathers know the importance of maintaining authority. Unlike mothers, they 'seldom threaten to punish; they usually do it on the spot' (Allen and Dickerson 2012, 114). Moreover, fathers have the advantage of not only being 'bigger and stronger', but they also do not 'become emotionally upset' (Passley 2006, 92). Mothers may cry or show that they are distressed, and this will be seen and exploited as weakness by the boy who 'recognize[s] that he has the upper hand with his weaker mother' (2006, 92).

In addition, fathers know the importance of meeting out punishments for the right kind of infractions, whereas mothers are likely to do it 'for every minor offence' (Estelle 2013, 15). However, since 'a father's voice carries a different weight', the child will likely obey anyway, obviating any need for punishment (Anderson 2017, 16).

Fathers are also better parents because they are fun to be with: they play with the children, think up exciting adventures and do things with the children. This harmonizes with Furstenberg's observation that 'fathers, even when they remain on the scene, play a recreational rather than instrumental role in their children's lives' (1988, 209). In the advice books, this is represented as a strength, a sign of fathers' superior qualities. Mothers are represented as obsessed with neatness, safety and boring tasks.

A recurring claim in many of the books, by female authors as well as male, is the importance of men. One of Dennis' informants makes the observation that '"all men are designed to be leaders … to take dominion over the whole earth"' (2015, 130). Small defines a 'real man' as someone who 'knows that his job as a father is to guide, guard and govern; direct, correct, and protect' (Small 2017, 103). Small stresses again and again that a father is supposed to be the head of the household; it is his task to lead his wife and his children. 'He is a guardian of his wife's virtue and has the ability to nurture and care for his children' (2017, 109). As is noted by Dowd, the nurture Small envisages is mainly as breadwinner and 'CEO': a father 'oversees the family operations, makes the decisions and sees that they are carried out' (2017, 149). There is no evidence that he expects a father to take any part in hands-on childcare, or in any housework. Certainly, a wife is expected to cook, clean and wash up (2017, 143). The fathering he envisages is Dowd's 'dominant mode' (2000, 22). Small, like so many of the other authors, is engaged in 'restoring fatherhood to the prominence it deserves' (Blankenhorn 2007, xi). In short, the advice books make a claim for what Dowd has noted as men's 'belief in their own uniqueness' which is required to give them 'a reason to connect with their children' (2000, 9). The advice books appear to suggest that it is not enough for a father to love and be loved by his child – his exceptionalism as a father, not just a parent, must be praised.

Apologists for absent fathers

The advice books argue for the absolute necessity to have at least some form of father substitute around. Yet some of them warn against stepfathers, reiterating the danger stepfathers are assumed to pose to young boys that Marsiglio and Pleck have found expressed in some of the academic debates on fatherhood (2005, 250). The advice authors do have to admit that in some cases, fathers just do not want to be with their children, but they make it clear that they are not out to make these fathers feel bad. Several state that what they have written is not a 'father-bashing' book (e.g., Tardy 2006, 13).

One reason given for fathers staying away is that they feel ashamed that they cannot keep up with the child support payments. This is possibly linked to the ideal of men as breadwinners, that a real man supports his family. Child support payments are invariably presented as extortionate and unfair by male authors (see e.g. Bryant 2015; Dennis 2015; Lewis 2010). Bryant, who himself has spent time in prison for non-payment of child support, refers to women who seek legal help to obtain the payments as 'queens of the courthouse' and argues that their attempts to 'extract unreasonable financial supports' will make a father 'completely lose any desires of returning to his child' (22).[2] Allen and Dickerson even go so far as to suggest 'an attractive tax deduction' for fathers who agree to spend 'a specified number of days each year' with their own children (2012, 174). The father constructed here is one whose love is financially motivated. If staying in contact with the child costs too much, he will simply not bother.

Other reasons suggested for fathers staying away include feeling a lack of knowledge of how to interact with the children (Dennis 2015, 61). Bryant and Small see historical and racial reasons behind absent fathers. Bryant argues that Black men were not allowed 'to provide for themselves, much less a wife or child' (2015, 34). Small refers to three generations of Black men stuck in 'psychological adolescence' because of a lack of fathers (2017, 102).

Fathers may also stay away because they feel excluded. The solution for this is for mothers to 'encourage absent fathers' to be more involved with the child (Allen and Dickerson 2012, 71). Dennis, similarly, urges the mother to involve the father, using language that suggests maternal gatekeeping: 'Let him drop the kid off at school, let him take part in parent-teacher meetings' (2012, 60). The image of fathers constructed in the advice books can be summed up as one of physically and mentally strong, stable and competent role models who will guide their sons towards responsible adulthood, if they are only allowed by the children's gatekeeping mothers.

Counternarratives

A recurring topic in many of the books is the stern admonition to the mother that she must not 'trash' or 'talk-down' men in general and her son's father in particular (for instance, Leman 2006, 177). This does not stop a number of female authors, for example, Buchanan, Chisholm, Howland and Joyce, from making disparaging comments about their former husbands and how they failed to live up to their task as fathers. Pearson goes the furthest, for instance referring to the father of her child as the 'sperm donor' (2019, 9). Yet, even these authors, along with most of the others, place the biological father at the centre of the life of the heterosexual family. Although they address an audience that does not have that, this is the life they envisage for the children of the mother readers. However, in some of the books, there are hints of a counternarrative, of a different view of family life and childrearing. This counternarrative suggests that biological fathers are not best placed to raise sons, that a single mother is better on her own. As Panettieri asks, 'Is there actually anything a father provides that a mother cannot?' (2008, 6).

One way the single mother is better off is that she can make decisions about childrearing on her own, without any *'inconsistencies in the parenting and no one fight[ing] me over how to parent'* (Adams 2011, 24, 131, original italics). Howland relates how a married mother confesses to envy the fact that Howland makes all important decisions on her own, rather than having to 'fight and argue over what's best for your child' (2020, 198).

There are also references to fathers being poor parents. Unlike mothers, fathers will not sacrifice their own time or interests for their children; they are 'too busy or preoccupied to be involved with their sons (Meeker 2015, xviii). Panettieri criticizes fathers who spend less than five minutes a day with their children, 'where is the quality "fathering" so many experts insist is essential to a boy's healthy development?' (2008, 6). Chisholm suggests that simple paternal presence is not enough: 'what about the *quality* of male presence?' (2007, 27, original emphasis). Fathers may not notice when their sons are in emotional distress, or simply tell them to 'man up' (Meeker 2015, 28). Meeker further claims that men simply are not capable of helping a distraught son identify and deal with strong emotion (2015, 29). This is something only mothers can do. In fact, fathers may themselves be so damaged by the repressive masculinity afforded boys and men in American contemporary culture that they are unable to help their sons navigate the difficult world they are growing up in (2015, 30) or show closeness, love and affection (Panettieri 2008, 90).

Citing previous research, Marsiglio and Peck write that fathers tend to 'reproduce gender inequality', 'encourag[ing] masculine behaviors in sons' (2005, 257). Panettieri makes the same observation, noting that fathers will 'express alarm at what they perceive as inappropriate preferences in clothes, toys, or behavior' (2008, 30). Thus the single mother is fortunate, since she is not 'fighting to overcome restrictive thinking upon her son by a reactionary, threatened male' (2008, 30).

Male authors such as Dennis claim that men raised by women will become '"over-feminize[d] … and then they will be nothing"' (149). In particular, they will not be able to relate properly to women, since boys learn how to interact with girlfriends and wives from their fathers, not from their mothers (Allen and Dickerson 2012, 17). In the counternarrative, this is dismissed. Adams reports that 'studies show' that boys raised by single mothers relate better to women (2011, 175). Living with a single mother also allows for greater access to more adults, of both sexes. Panettieri maintains that 'maternal grandparents, aunts, uncles' can give a son more attention than one father (2008, 5). Engber and Klungness ask the question what happens 'when boys don't have one single, constant male' to model themselves on and answer that '[t]his might actually be a good thing' since the boy will 'not have just one role model, but the opportunity to have many' (2006, 277). Adams goes so far as to suggest that the father is an obstacle to the child's bonding with other adults; when he is gone: 'your former in-laws may have more of an opportunity to become involved' (2011, 125). The image constructed here is of the heterosexual family as a claustrophobic space where sons are only given one, potentially damaging, or at least limiting, male role model. As Engber and Klungness state, a 'father at home who does not provide the necessary qualities of a healthy male role model can do more harm than good' (2006, 277). The single mother, if she has a wide social network, affords the child a much healthier environment. However, the need for male role models is not questioned even in this narrative.

This counternarrative can be seen as a new departure, but the end result is a greater burden on mothers. As Panettieri asks, 'what can moms do to change the course of male relationships' so that their sons 'can have deep, meaningful, and satisfying relationships with their own families?' (2008, 90). Since biological fathers cannot be relied upon to help their sons grow up in a troubled world, it falls on the mothers to do that. Only mothers have the ability. Meg Meeker, for example, referencing the 'boy crisis', claims that 'the means to resolving this crisis often lie in the mother's hands' (2015, xvi). As Barnett and Rivers write when discussing cultural notions of women's greater sensitivity, this idea 'not only takes men off the hook but puts an impossible burden on women' (2005, 22). The mother reader is assured by the counternarrative that not having a biological father in the household may not be a problem after all, but it is now up to her to solve all the problems, for example, through organizing playdates, liaising with schools and finding the right role models.

Fathers Raising Daughters

Having analysed the way mothers are discursively constructed by the advice books aimed at single mothers, I now turn to advice books written for single fathers raising daughters to see how they construct these fathers, using the same websites as for the books aimed at mothers to find material. This is not intended to be an exhaustive analysis, but rather a brief overview, as a contrast to the main analysis. However, I have managed to find only one book with a specific focus on single fathers raising daughters (Gross and Livingston 2012). The other books are either about single fathers in general or about fathers raising daughters, but not necessarily on their own as primary caregivers. This may reflect the fact that the number of father-headed single-parent households is considerably smaller than mother-headed ones in the United States, and so the market for advice books aimed at such fathers is smaller.[3] There are also books like R. C. Blakes' *The Father-Daughter Talk* (2014), which is not so much an advice book on raising a daughter as a list of dangers in contemporary society that a young girl should avoid, such as multiple sex partners, drugs or alcohol. In the end, I have chosen to focus on 10 books: one book by two men, one book by two women, two books by a man and a woman, one book a female author and five books by male authors. Two of the books are written by authors whose mother-son books are part of my main analysis: Meg Meeker and Kevin Leman. To the best of my knowledge, only two books are by Black authors. See the appendix for more information.

One of the most striking differences between the two groups of books I have analysed lies in the motivation for writing and the reader's address. Whereas many of the books aimed at single mothers begin with an assumption of the mothers' insufficiency – that without help from the books and male role models, the readers' sons will suffer from poor grades, drug and alcohol abuse, depression and suicide – many of the books aimed at fathers take their importance as the starting point. The authors note that a father makes an 'indelible imprint' on his daughter's life (Leman 2017) or list the '52 things daughters need from their dads' (Payleitner 2013). Meg Meeker reassures the father readers that they 'are good men who have been derided by a culture that does not care for you', a culture that has 'ridiculed your authority' and 'denied your importance' and devotes an entire chapter to explaining that the father must be a hero to his daughter (2015, xiii).[4] In short, the books specifically addressing fathers of young daughters, often teenagers, make it clear to the father reader that he is a very important figure in his daughter's life, and it is through his influence that she will grow up confident and strong, avoiding eating disorders, sexual abuse, self-harm or academic failure (Meeker 2017, 2).

The difference in attitude towards paternal and maternal expertise and suitability as a parent and a role model is exemplified by Edwards (2020) and Howland (2020). Both authors address the problems of raising a teenager. Edwards describes the various strategies and measures he has taken in order to turn his stepdaughter into 'a well-adjusted, hardworking, honest, confident, young adult' (2020, 3). There is no suggestion in the book that a father is not emotionally or physically equipped to raise a daughter into a woman. Howland, on the other hand, writes about how she realized that she could not raise her teenage son to be a man and describes her strategies for finding four male mentors, who have helped her son come out of the 'jungle of adolescence a gentleman and a warrior' (2020, 215).

Some books use the strategy, also observed by Courtney in her study of domestic advice books for men, of appealing to the masculinity of the reader (2009). Mike Klumpp, for example, devotes a chapter of his *The Single Dad's Survival Guide: How to Succeed as a One-Man Parenting Team* to the claim that 'This Job Calls for a Man', in which he stresses to the father reader that '*you've got to be a man*' (2003, 3, original emphasis). Being a man in this context is to draw on the particular abilities men supposedly have: 'strength, leadership, discipline, vision, and organization' (2003, 3). This is a form of reader address that is rarely, if ever, used in books aimed at mothers.

Most of the books that are aimed at single fathers, whether of daughters or children in general, tend towards a more measured tone, focusing on practicalities such as how to deal with legal issues (Baird 2011), cooking and cleaning (Shimberg and Shimberg 2007) and how to maintain contact with the children whilst travelling or being deployed overseas (Ashley and Hall 2008). Gross and Livingston (2012) also urge the father reader to make sure that he can help his daughter with purchasing bras and explain that it is his responsibility to learn about sanitary pads and tampons (2012, 49). This can be contrasted to Dennis, who in support of his claim that only men can raise boys, emphatically states that he is not able to help his daughter to choose the best form of hygiene products, since 'DAD DOESN'T KNOW! … I don't even want know!' (2015, 31).

Unlike the books aimed at mothers, none of the authors suggest that a divorced or widowed father should not go on dates. Instead, it is assumed that not only are fathers expected to date, but they are allowed to not be 'looking for anything serious' (Edwards, 2020, 145). Gross and Livingston even suggest that the father reader might want to have casual sexual liaisons without intending to marry, 'a little intimacy with no real strings attached' (2012, 105) and give advice on how to do this without it affecting the daughter. This stands in stark contrast to the advice books for mothers, which only accept dating if it is with the intention of marriage, and certainly do not allow casual relationships. Anderson even goes so far as to claim that if the son sees his mother have different boyfriends, he will lose his respect, not only for her, but for women in general (2017, 33–34). As he writes, '[b]ecoming a parent is a life of sacrifice' and that includes sacrificing the right to a sex life (2017, 34). Comparing the two groups of books, it is clear that it is only mothers who are expected to make this particular kind of sacrifice.

In sum, the advice books aimed at (single) fathers follow the general cultural pattern that fathers are praised for even the simplest acts of childrearing or are excused as well-meaning, if bumbling.[5] They may need to be taught why it is important to have a clean house (Ashley and Hall, 2008), but they are trying their best. In addition, the advice books iterate the message that fathers are vital to the child's maturity and growth, be it a boy or a girl. This could be in response to the reality that although men are spending more time with their children than previously, they are still a long way behind mothers (Dowd 2000), so the books can be read as an attempt at persuading fathers to take a more hands-on interest in their children. Looking at all the advice books I have analysed, those aimed at mothers and those aimed at fathers, their message can be summed up as the idea that boys must be rescued *from* their mothers, whereas girls need to be rescued *by* their fathers. In short, to be a mummy's boy is a recipe for social disaster and might even lead to an early death, whereas to be a daddy's girl is a prerequisite for personal and social success.

Chapter 5

CONCLUSION

Advice books cover a plethora of topics, suggesting many ways in which the reader can become richer, cleverer, thinner, happier, more focused and less stressed. The books may promise to help readers put painful experiences or habits behind them or teach them new skills. These books intend to help the readers become better versions of themselves. But this is not the message broadcast by advice books aimed at (single) mothers raising sons. Whereas the general self-help book will reassure readers that although they suffer from a lack, this lack can be resolved, the most a mother of a son can do is stop inappropriate or harmful behaviour, such as shouting, belittling or smothering the boy. But she cannot teach the boy how to become a man, and so she needs to find suitable role models for him.

Sandra Dolby, in her analysis of the genre of advice books, refers to it as a form of urban legend, in the way that it may keep 'certain beliefs, customs, attitudes, and stereotypes alive' (2005, 10). This is also what happens in the advice books. The ideas that mothers are incapable of understanding and appreciating boy behaviour, that boys must put their mothers behind and enter the world of men through fathers or father figures are repeated again and again. Another stereotype repeated is that through their inept parenting, single mothers are responsible for the disintegration of contemporary society, since boys who are not raised correctly will turn into criminals, mass shooters and terrorists. There are different voices, of course, inflected through the prism of gender, class and race. For example, some authors are in favour of mothers working, whereas others promote staying at home while the children are young, or at least working from home. Some authors help with legal terminology, which might be useful if a son has been arrested. Others give advice on the importance of music lessons.

People turn to advice books for a number of reasons, as Nicolas Marquis remarks in his study of readers' response to French advice books (2019). Moreover, what they choose to take away from the book varies and may not even be what the author intended. This is evident when looking at Amazon reviews of some of the books I have analysed. Meg Meeker's *Strong Mothers,*

Strong Sons (2015) is one of the highest selling parenting books on Amazon and has, at the time of writing, 1 882 ratings, with an average of 4.7 stars out of 5. One reviewer, Angel, has given the book five stars and writes that the 'book saved me' (2019). On the other end, a reader calling herself Amazon Customer gives the book only one star, writing that rather than relying on evidence, the book uses a 'fear-based approach to parenting' and warns against buying it (2020). These readers choose for themselves whether to follow the advice or not. More troubling is perhaps Molasses' response to Bay Buchanan's *Bay and Her Boys* (2012). In the book, Buchanan stresses very strongly that a single mother must not date any man or harbour hopes of (re)marrying until her children are grown. Molasses writes that reading this 'made me feel so guilty' and that she was 'overwhelmed with sorrow' since she would very much like to find a new husband (2013). In her comments, she pleads her case for wanting a new husband and asks whether she is 'such a terrible person to want such things' (2013). Unlike the reader Amazon Customer, who simply chooses to reject the author's advice, Molasses appears to feel bound by it, accepting Buchanan as an authority that must be obeyed.

What can be said of most of the books I have analysed is that they do not appear to be in step with a great deal of public conversations about parenting and what constitutes a family. Professor of Sociology Barbara Katz Rothman, for example, notes that single motherhood has become 'a perfectly ordinary way to raise children' (2009, 324). Fathers protest against ads that present them as inept parents to such an extent that companies are forced to change their advertising campaigns (Belkin 2012). US family structures are becoming increasingly diverse, featuring same-sex parents, single parents by choice as well as more sprawling family structures that allow for a wider meaning of the concept of family (Casper and Bianchi 2002; Golombok 2015). In popular culture, non-normative family structures are showcased, such as in the sitcoms *Oh Baby* (1998–2000), *One Big Happy* (2015) and *Modern Family* (2009–2020), which depict same-sex parents as well as single mothers by choice who use ARTs to conceive. Although some of these depictions have been criticized for reproducing conservative stereotypes (Cavalcante 2015; Pugh 2018), the fact that these programmes are produced and viewed demonstrates a wider acceptance of more diverse family structures, at least to the point that money can be made from it. And yet, the advice books aimed at single mothers continue to be published by major publishing houses, smaller presses as well as authors using self-publishing platforms. Evidently, the books fulfil a need for some authors and readers, which suggests that there is a continued need for conversations about parenthood and what kinds of futures we want for our children.

APPENDIX

Mothers raising sons.

Author Name	Additional Information Given	Race
Adams, Janis	Author, blogger, columnist. Single mother, one child.	White
Allen, Mardi	PhD, psychologist.	White
Anderson, Antonio D.	BA in Criminal Justice, MDiv. Pastor, social worker.	Black
Biddulph. Steve	Psychologist.	White
Bolds, Denise	Master of Social Work.	Black
Bourne, Jr., Mervin A.	JD, lawyer. Son of a single mother. Website: www.mervinbourne.com .	Black
Boyd-Franklin, Nancy	PhD, psychologist. Married, one biological and three step-children.	Black
Bromfield, Richard	PhD, clinical psychologist. Married, two children.	White
Bryant, Christopher K.	Founder of Hillman B2. Single. Non-residential father, one child.	Black
Buchanan, Bay	MA in mathematics. Former United States Treasurer. Single mother, three children.	White
Chisholm, Dana	MA in organizational leadership. Single mother, two children.	White
Dennis, John P.	Formerly in the US Air Force, now working in the corporate sector. Divorced, non-residential father, remarried, three children.	Black
Dickerson, James L.	Author, journalist, social worker. Divorced, non-residential father.	White
Elium, Don	MFT, marriage, family and child counsellor. Married, two children.	White
Elium, Jeanne	Writer, university instructor, elementary school teacher. Married, two children.	White
Engber, Andrea	Single mother, one child.	White
Erwin, Cheryl	MA. Marriage and family therapist. Has a family.	White
Estelle, Khaz	Novelist, poet, essayist. Son of a single mother.	Black
Franklin, A. J.	PhD, psychologist. Divorced, co-parenting father, remarried. Four children.	Black
Hall, Philip S.	PhD in psychology, licensed school psychologist.	White

(Continued)

(*Continued*)

Author Name	Additional Information Given	Race
Howland, MaryAnne	Founder and CEO of Ibis Communications, www.ibiscommunications.com	Black
Johnson, Rick	Author, founder of Better Dads, www.betterdadsnet. Married, two children.	White
Joyce, Donna	Single, mother, divorced, one child.	Unknown
Kennedy, Neil	Founder of FivestarMan, www.fivestarman.com. Son of a single, remarried woman. Married, children.	White
Klungness, Leah	PhD, psychologist.	White
Krause, Tina	Freelance writer, editor, newspaper columnist. Married, two children.	White
King, Darrell W.	Minister, author, executive producer, former youth pastor. Founder and CEO of The Missing Man, Inc. Son of a single mother.	Black
Leman, Kevin	PhD, psychologist. Founder of the Leman Academy of Excellence. Married, five children.	White
Lewis, Franklin Donny D.	Has worked with youth in the LA Probation Department and group homes. Son of a single mother. Non-residential single father.	Black
Meeker, Meg	MD. Married, four children.	White
Moffitt, Betina	Single, divorced mother. One child.	Black
Moore, Derrick	Developmental Coach and Football Team Chaplain for the Georgia Institute of Technology. Married, three children.	Black
Moore, Stephanie Perry	Author, co-executive editor for the Sisters in Faith Bible and general editor for Nia Publishing. Married, three children. Website: www.stephanieperrymoore.com	Black
Norwood, Lisa	Supervisor in the Juvenile Court System. Founder of Mothers Raising Sons, Inc. Single mother, three children. Website: https://mothersraisingsons.org/	Black
Palmer, Shondreka	Certified personal trainer, certified health and wellness coach. Single mother, one child. Website: https://executefithealth.com.	Black
Panettieri, Gina	Literary agent, president of Talcott Notch Literary Services. Single mother, three children.	White
Passley, Josef A.	PhD in Clinical Psychology.	Black
Pearson, Jenieka L.	Associate degree in business. Single mother, three children.	Black
Phillips, Patrick	MSW, author, national speaker, educator. Son of a single mother. Married, one child. Website: www.mrphillipsinspires.com.	Black
Small, William	PhD in Religious Studies, chairman/CEO of Beautiful Ministries, Inc. Married, children.	Black
Stoppe, Rhonda	Christian speaker. Married, four children.	White
Swanson Monica	Author and blogger. Married, four children.	White
Tardy, Cederick W.	Son of a single mother. Naval MP.	Black
Tyler, Jamie	Married, three children.	White
Watkins, Deborah	Corrections counsellor. Single mother, two children.	Black

Fathers raising daughters.

Author name	Additional information given	Race
Ashley, Steven	Founder of the Divorced Fathers Network.	White
Baird, Craig	Spends time with his wife and their dogs and writes from home.	Unknown
Blakes Jr., R. C.	Senior Pastor of the New Home Family Worship Center in New Orleans, Louisiana, and Houston, Texas. Married, three daughters and a son.	Black
Edwards, Brian	Stepfather of one daughter.	Black
Gross, Gretchen	Clinical instructor in the Department of Psychiatry at the University of Vermont College of Medicine.	White
Hall, Philip S.	PhD in Psychology.	White
Klumpp, Mike	Writer, martial arts instruction, former pastor. Widower, remarried. Four children.	White
Leman, Kevin	Internationally known psychologist, radio and television personality, speaker and educator. Married, five children and four grandchildren.	White
Livingston, Patricia	Women's health nurse practitioner at the University of Vermont Center for Health and Wellbeing's Women's Health Clinic.	White
Meeker, Meg	More than 30 years practicing paediatric and adolescent medicine. Works with the NFL Fatherhood Initiative. Married, four children.	White
Payleitner, Jay	Freelance writer, ad man, motivational speaker and radio producer. Former Executive Director for the Illinois Fatherhood Initiative. Married, four sons, one daughter.	White
Shimberg, Elaine Fantle	Award-winning author of more than 20 books. Has written numerous articles on family issues, for example, *Reader's Digest*, *Woman's Day*, *Men's Health*. Member of the advisory board for the website KidsGrowth.com. www.thecompletesinglefather.com.	White
Shimberg, Michael	Son of Elaine Fantle Shimberg. Divorced father of two. Certified financial planner. www.thecompletesinglefather.com.	White

NOTES

Chapter 1

1. I have chosen to focus on advice books written for single mothers raising sons specifically, rather than sons and daughters. The reason for this is that advice books present the mother–son dynamic as particularly problematic, both on a personal and a societal level. There are many books addressing this problem, whereas there are few titles specifically targeting mothers of daughters, usually referring only to teenage daughters. And titles aimed at *single* mothers raising daughters are even fewer. The consensus seems to be that mothers do not need advice on how to raise their daughters and so there is no market for such books. Overall, girls are not perceived to be a problem the way boys are and so there is no need for books on how to raise them.
2. See, for example, the YouTube channel *Mediocre Tutorials and Reviews*, which posted a video analysing and agreeing with James' claims on 8 December 2020, https://www.youtube.com/watch?v=3EFAbzTXo0U.
3. Krafchick et al. label parenting books 'the largest category of self-help resources' (2005, 85).
4. I have limited this study to American material, but it is worth noting that these books have a potential global impact. Although they are written for the national market, some authors, such as Meg Meeker, have also been translated into other languages, such as Italian, French, Spanish, German and Chinese (Amazon website). The American advice books are also made available, in English, to an international readership through online bookshops. To give one example closer to home, several of the books in my corpus are available in Sweden, in English. Although the social, legal and financial situation of Swedish single mothers is very different from that of American mothers (Wahlström Henriksson and Bergnehr 2021), the American advice books apparently have a readership in Sweden and may thus have an impact on the way Swedish single mothers regard themselves and are regarded by others.
5. Scholars appear to use the terms 'advice book' and 'self-help book' interchangeably. See for example Nakamura's 'English Parenting for Japanese Parents: A Critical Review of Advice in Self-Help Books for Raising Bilingual Children in Japan' (2021) and Sandretto and Nairn's 'Do Parenting Advice Books Help or Harm? Critiquing "Common-Sense" Advice for Mothers Raising Boys' (2019). I have opted for the term 'advice book' mainly to underscore the connection to advice books aimed at mothers in previous centuries. For a discussion on the difficulty of delimiting self-help/advice books from other types of literature, see Marquis (2019).
6. For an extensive study of advice books regulating women, see Barbara Ehrenreich and Deirdre English, *For Her Own Good: Two Centuries of the Experts' Advice to Women* (2005).

7. Although both men are listed as authors on the cover, it is made clear in the book that Gray is the author of only one section, on ADHD. Farrell writes from a first-person perspective, referring to his position as adviser to the President of the United States and driving force behind a number of national initiatives intended to help boys.
8. For an insightful discussion of how suicide amongst young men is used as a rhetorical strategy to legitimize claims of a war on boys, without taking other factors into consideration, see Allan (2015). He points out that 'the queer boy, the boy of color, the queer boy of color, and so on are affected by any number of identities' and that 'being male is not the cause of suicide' (2015, 30). Likewise, one should be wary of claiming that being fatherless is necessarily the cause of suicide.
9. Farrell's book has a very impressive reference section, which supposedly supports his statements about, for example, brain development, emotional development and innate skills. However, when examining the sources for some of the most surprising claims, I found them all to be either incorrectly applied or less relevant. A great many refer to statistics that are up to 40 years old. Some articles do not discuss what Farrell argues they do. Others detail research on very limited cohorts or children in different places/socioeconomic circumstances, such as a study of 497 Dutch, mainly White, middle-class children (283 boys and 231 girls) as regards empathy (Van der Graaff et al. 2014). One of the results of the study is that social constraints may cause teenage boys to pretend not to care about other people's emotions (2014, 888). Farrell uses the study to support sweeping, biological claims concerning teenage boys in general (2018, 263). In another instance, Farrell references a study of 300 self-selected men in Toronto (2018, 250). In the article itself, the authors state emphatically that their research should not be extrapolated 'to the general population' but instead used as 'a springboard to further investigation' (Bollinger and Van How 2011, 192). Although admitting that it is a preliminary study, Farrell still maintains that the results suggest a 20 per cent chance that the reader's son might suffer the ill effects investigated in the study (2018, 250).
10. US Census statistics show that the number of children living with a single mother has decreased steadily since 2012 (Statista 2021).
11. As Lisa D. Brush has shown, there is a strict hierarchy in terms of the perceived respectability of single mothers, with widows at the top and unwed mothers at the bottom (1997).
12. The one exception is Howland, who includes a section on how her son was allowed to meet Barack Obama (2020).

Chapter 2

1. Its shape even makes it hard to delimit it from the surrounding tissue, making claims about sex-based differences in size difficult to support (Fausto-Sterling 2000, 119).
2. Fine quotes one popularizing text in which the authors write that MRI means 'see[ing] your brain operating live on a television screen' (2010, 134).
3. For a summary and discussion of a number of the points raised, see Lucas Gottzén (2018).
4. The one exception is Biddulph, who devotes one page to 'Boys Who Want to Be Girls' (2015, 136). He reassures the reader that this is 'not connected to homosexuality' and refers to a study in which the boys 'outgrew the "disorder" by late adolescence' (2015, 136).

5. Panettieri does not give a complete reference. The study that comes closest to her description concerns the shape and size of bones in the inner ear. Carried out on 18 subjects between the ages of 1 day and 76 years, it established that there was a degree of sexual dimorphism in cochlear length. Coupling this with 'reports' of differences in 'pure-tone auditory sensitivity' between men and women, the authors make the tentative suggestion that there may be anatomic reasons for this difference in auditory sensitivity (Sato, Sando, and Takahashi 1991, 1039). There is a long leap from this potential difference to boys being unable to hear, or unwilling to listen to, their mothers.
6. Meeker includes an anecdote where she suggests to an adult man that his single mother is to blame for the herpes he contracted as a teenager and later gave to his wife. He thinks about it and agrees: '"Hell yes … we didn't talk about sex"' (2015, 252).

Chapter 3

1. Hays notes the racial affiliation of a few mothers, for example, one Latina and one African Brazilian mother, but does not address this in her analysis.
2. Tyler's book does not have page numbers.
3. Buchanan suggests that the mother reader consider whether she can 'trade in the fancy car for a cheaper used one' (2012, 52).
4. The most striking example is Buchanan, who describes how cheaply she was able to take her children to Yosemite (only $100 dollars for camping) only to note in passing that she brought the nanny with them.
5. No mother reader is instructed to seek help from her imam.

Chapter 4

1. For an extensive but concise description and synthesis, see Elizabeth Podnieks (2016).
2. Those female authors who mention child support all urge the mother reader to make sure that the boy receives what he is owed (for instance Panettieri 2008, 116).
3. In 2020, according to the US Census, 3.27 million children were living with a single father, whereas 15.31 million were living with a single mother (Statista 2021).
4. This book, first published in 2006, was followed in 2017 by *You've Got This: Unlocking the Hero Dad Within*.
5. Klumpp retells as a humorous anecdote how he failed to realize that his daughter was entering puberty and had not prepared with any sanitary towels of tampons: 'I just didn't happen to have any tampons lying around the house to give her. But I could give her personal attention and love' (2003, 57). This kind of forgiving attitude is not evidenced in any of the books aimed at single mothers.

BIBLIOGRAPHY

Primary sources

Books for mothers

Adams, Janis. 2011. *A Complete Guide for Single Moms: Everything You Need to Know About Raising Healthy, Happy Children on Your Own*. Ocala, FL: Atlantic Publishing Group.
Allen, Mardi, and James L. Dickerson. 2012. *Sons without Fathers: What Every Mother Needs to Know*. Jackson, MS: Sartoris Literary Group.
Anderson, Antonio D. 2017. *7 Successful Principles for Single Mothers Raising Sons*. Lulu Publishing Services.
Biddulph, Steve. 2015. *Raising Boys: Why Boys Are Different and How to Help Them Becoming Happy and Well-balanced Men*. 3rd edition. London: Harper Thorsons.
Bolds, Denise. 2008. *Raising Princes to be Kings: A Single Black Mother's Guide to Raising Her Black Sons*. Poughkeepsie.
Bourne Jr., Mervin A. 2016. *A Single Mother's Guide to Raising a Son*. Mervin A. Bourne Jr.
Boyd-Franklin, Nancy, and A. J. Franklin. 2001. *Boys into Men: Raising Our African American Teenage Sons*. New York: Plume.
Bromfield, Richard, and Cheryl Erwin. 2001. *How to Turn Boys into Men Without a Man Around the House: A Single Mother's Guide*. Roseville: Prima Publishing.
Bryant, Christopher K. 2015. *An Open Letter to My Son: Lessons for Sons of Single Mothers*. Atlanta: Christopher K. Bryant.
Buchanan, Bay. 2012. *Bay and Her Boys: Unexpected Lessons I Learned as a (Single) Mom*. Cambridge, MA: Da Capo Lifelong.
Chisholm, Dana S. 2007. *Single Moms Raising Sons: Preparing Boys to Be Men When There's No Man Around*. Kansas City: Beacon Hill Press.
Dennis, John. 2015. *Men Raised by Women: What He Won't Tell Mom*. John P. Dennis.
Elium, Don and Jeanne Elium. 2004. *Raising as Son*. 3rd edition. Berkeley: Celestial Arts.
Engber, Andrea, and Leah Klungness. 2006. *The Complete Single Mother*. Avon, MA: Adams Media.
Estelle, K. 2013. *The 7 Principles for Raising Black Sons: A Practical Hand-Guide for Today's Single Black Mothers*. Next Level Publications Incorporated.
Howland, MaryAnne. 2020. *Warrior Rising: How Four Men Helped a Boy on His Journey to Manhood*. New York: Tarcher Perigee.
Johnson, Rick. 2011. *That's My Teenage Son: How Moms Can Influence Their Boys to Become Good Men*. Grand Rapids: Revell.
Jones, LaVeda M. 2015. *'Raising a Prince Without a King': A Single Mother's Journey to Victory*. Love Clones, Inc.

Joyce, Donna. 2018. *Single Moms Raising Boys. Vol. 2.* Donna Joyce.
Kennedy, Neil. 2014. *A Mother's Guide to Raising a Fivestarman: Training Your Son to Respect You, Himself, and Others and Grow into the Five Passions of Authentic Manhood.* CreateSpace Independent Publishing Platform.
King, Darrell W. 2015. *7 Things Every Mother Should Teach Her Son.* Get Knowledge Books.
Krause, Tina. 2014. *The Savvy Mom's Guide to Sons: 101 Real-World Tips to Improve Your Relationship and Save Your Sanity.* Uhrichsville, OH: Shiloh Run Press.
Leman, Kevin. 2006. *Single Parenting That Works: Six Keys to Raising Happy, Healthy Children in a Single-Parent Home.* Tyndale House Publishers.
Lewis, Franklin Donny D. 2010. *Single Mother's Guide to Raising Black Boys.* XLibris.
Meeker, Meg. 2015. *Strong Mothers, Strong Sons: Lessons Mothers Need to Raise Extraordinary Men.* New York: Ballantine Books.
Moffitt, Betina. 2020. *Raising a Boy into a Man: A Mother's Journey After Divorce.* Fiery Beacon Publishing House, LLC.
Moore, Derrick, and Stephanie Perry Moore. 2013. *Raise Him Up: A Single Mother's Guide to Raising a Successful Black Man.* Nashville: Thomas Nelson.
Norwood, Lisa. 2016. *The Manual: Real Life Testimonies & Advice from Mothers & Sons.* Ellenwood: Mother Raising Sons, Inc.
Palmer, Shondreka. 2013. *Independently Raising a Man: Thoughts from a Single Mother's Perspective.* CreateSpace Independent Publishing Platform.
Panettieri, Gina, and Philip S. Hall. 2008. *The Single Mother's Guide to Raising Remarkable Boys.* Avon, MA: Adams Media.
Passley, Josef A. 2006. *Single Parenting in the 21st Century and Beyond: A Single Mother's Guide to Rearing Sons Without Fathers.* Oxford: Trafford Publishing.
Pearson, Jenieka L. 2019. *Rise Before the Son: Advice for Single Mothers on Raising Successful Boys.* Bloomington, IN: iUniverse.
Phillips, Patrick. 2018. *Don't Just Love Your Son...Raise Him: 15 Thought Provoking Questions for Single Moms Raising Sons.* Akron: Ohio Education Empowerment Group, LLC.
Small, William C. 2017. *Single Mothers and Sons: A Journey into Manhood.* Dallas: First World Publishing.
Stoppe, Rhonda. 2013. *Moms Raising Sons to Be Men.* Eugene, OR: Harvest House Publishers.
Swanson, Monica. 2019. *Boy Mom: What Your Son Needs Most from You.* New York: WaterBrook.
Tardy, Cederick W. 2006. *The Big Payback: A Guide on Raising a Young Man as a Single Mother from the Perspective of a Young Man.* Houston: Cederick Tardy Enterprises.
Tyler, Jamie. 2014. *Parenting for Single Mothers: Being A Good Mom and Raising Great Kids.* USA: CreateSpace Publishing Platform.
Watkins, Deborah. 2017. *Some Will Be King Makers: A Single Mother's Journey Raising African American Males.* Buffalo: M2M Publishing.

Books for fathers

Ashley, Steven and Philip S. Hall. (2008). *The Long-Distance Dad: How You Can Be There for Your Child – Whether Divorced, Deployed or on the Road.* Avon: Adams Media.
Baird, Craig. (2011). *A Complete Guide for Single Dads: Everything You Need to Know About Raising Healthy, Happy Children On Your Own.* Atlantic Publishing Group Inc.
Blakes Jr., R. C. and Rachel Blakes. (2014). *The Father-Daughter Talk.* Pearland: Untapped Potential.

Edwards, Brian. (2020). *Raising a Teenage Daughter as a Single Dad: The Roller Coaster Ride with My Self-Obsessed, Moody and Defiant Daughter.* Outskirts Press.

Gross, Gretchen and Patricia Livingston. (2020). *But Dad! A Survival Guide for Single Fathers of Tween and Teen Daughters.* Lanham: Rowman & Littlefield.

Klumpp, Mike. (2003). *The Single Dad's Survival Guide: How to Succeed as a One-Man Parenting Team.* Colorado Springs: WaterBrook Press.

Leman, Kevin. (2017). *Be the Dad She Needs You to Be: The Indelible Imprint a Father Leaves on His Daughter's Life.* Nashville: Thomas Nelson.

Meeker, Meg. 2006. *Strong Fathers, Strong Daughters: 10 Secrets Every Father Should Know.* Simon and Schuster.

Payleitner, Jay. 2013. *52 Things Daughters Need from Their Dads.* Eugene: Harvest House Publishers.

Shimberg, Elaine Fantle and Michael Shimberg. 2007. *The Complete Single Father: Reassuring Answers to Your Most Challenging Situations.* Adams Media.

Secondary sources

Adair, Vyvyan. 2000. *From Good Ma to Welfare Queen: The Poor Woman in American Literature, Photography, and Culture.* New York: Garland Publishing.

Adams, Kenneth. 2007. *When He's Married to Mom: How to Help Mother-Enmeshed Men Open Their Hearts to True Love and Commitment.* New York: Fireside.

Adams, Michele, and Scott Coltrane. 2005. 'Boys and Men in Families'. In *Handbook of Studies on Men and Masculinities,* edited by Michael S. Kimmel, Jeff Hearn and Raewyn Connell, 230–248. Thousand Oaks, CA: SAGE Publications.

Allan, Jonathan A. 2015. 'No Future for Boys?'. *Boyhood Studies* 8 (1):22–33.

Amazon, Customer. 2020. 'Fear-mongering, Heteronormative, Christian, Conservative'. Amazon, accessed 28 Feb. https://www.amazon.com/gp/customer-reviews/R1PQO8UB67P0YO/ref=cm_cr_dp_d_rvw_ttl?ie=UTF8&ASIN=0345518101.

Anderson, Kristina J., and Christina Accomando. 2002. '"Real" Boys? Manufacturing Masculinity and Erasing Privilege in Popular Books on Raising Boys'. *Feminism & Psychology* 12 (4):491–516.

Anderson, Kristina J., Jessica George, and Jessica Nease. 2002. 'Requirements, Risks, and Responsibility: Mothering and Fathering in Books about Raising Boys'. *Analysis of Social Issues and Public Policy* 2 (1):205–221.

Angel. 2019. 'Review'. Amazon, accessed 28 Feb. https://www.amazon.com/gp/customer-reviews/RTDQPX0L6VIHV/ref=cm_cr_dp_d_rvw_ttl?ie=UTF8&ASIN=0345518101.

Apple, Rima D. 2006. *Perfect Motherhood: Science and Childrearing in America.* London: Rutgers University Press.

Armengol-Carrera, Josep M. 2008. 'Where are Fathers in American Literature? Re-visiting Fatherhood in U.S. Literary History'. *The Journal of Men's Studies* 16 (2):211–226.

Åström, Berit. 2015a. '"Sucking the Corrupte Mylke of an Infected Nurse': Regulating the Dangerous Maternal Body'. *Journal of Gender Studies* 24 (5):574–586.

Åström, Berit. 2015b. 'A Narrative of Fear: Advice to Mothers'. *Literature and Medicine* 33 (1):113–131.

Åström, Berit. 2017. 'Marginalizing Motherhood: Postfeminist Fathers and Dead Mothers in Animated Films'. In *The Absent Mother in the Cultural Imagination: Missing, Presumed Dead,* edited by Berit Åström, 241–258. Basingstoke: Palgrave Macmillan.

Åström, Berit. 2021. 'Advice Books for Single Mothers Raising Sons: Biology, Culture and Guilt'. In *Single Parents: Representations and Resistance in an International Context*, edited by Berit Åström and Disa Bergnehr. London: Palgrave Macmillan.

Barnett, Rosalind, and Caryl Rivers. 2005. *Same Difference: How Gender Myths Are Hurting Our Relationship, Our Children, and Our Jobs*. New York: Basic Books.

Bauman, Zygmunt. 2001. *The Individualized Society*. Cambridge: Polity Press.

Beasley, Chris. 2012. 'Problematizing Contemporary Men/Masculinities Theorizing: The Contribution of Raewyn Connell and Conceptual-Terminological Tensions Today'. *The British Journal of Sociology* 63 (4):747–765.

Beasley, Chris. 2015. 'Caution! Hazards Ahead: Considering the Potential Gap between Feminist Thinking and Men/Masculinities Theory and Practice'. *Journal of Sociology* 51 (3):566–581.

Belkin, Lisa. 2012. 'Huggies Pulls Ads After Insulting Dads'. *Huffington Post*. Accessed 28 Feb, 2022. https://www.huffpost.com/entry/huggies-pulls-diaper-ads_b_1339074.

Berggren, Kalle. 2014. 'Sticky Masculinity: Post-Structuralism, Phenomenology and Subjectivity in Critical Studies on Men'. *Men and Masculinities* 17 (3):231–252.

Biddulph, Steve. 2015. *Raising Boys: Why Boys Are Different and How to Help Them Becoming Happy and Well-balanced Men*. 3rd edition. London: Harper Thorsons.

Blankenhorn, David. 1996. *Fatherless America: Confronting Our Most Urgent Social Problem*. New York: HarperPerennial.

Blankenhorn, David. 2007. *The Future of Marriage*. New York: Encounter Books.

Bollinger, Dan, and Roberts S. Van How. 2011. 'Alexithymia and Circumcision Trauma: A Preliminary Investigation'. *International Journal of Men's Health* 10 (2):184–195.

Brannen, Julia, and Ann Nilsen. 2005. 'Individualisation, Choice and Structure: a Discussion of Current Trends in Sociological Analysis'. *The Sociological Review* 53 (3):412–428.

Bridges, Tristan, and C. J. Pascoe. 2019. 'Hybrid Masculinities: New Directions in the Sociology of Men and Masculinities'. In *Gender through the Prism of Difference*, edited by Maxine Baca Zinn, Pierrette Hondagneu-Sotelo, Michael A. Messner and Stephanie Nawyn, 204–216. New York: Oxford University Press.

Brush, Lisa D. 1997. 'Worthy Widows, Welfare Cheats: Proper Womanhood in Expert Needs Talk about Single Mothers in the United States, 1900 to 1988'. *Gender & Society* 11 (6):720–746.

Butler, Judith. 1999. *Gender Trouble: Feminism and the Subversion of Identity*. New York: Routledge.

Cadogan, William. 1757. *An Essay upon Nursing and the Management of Children from their Birth to Three Years of Age*. London.

Caliendo, Stephen M, and Charlton D. McIlwain. 2021b. 'Introduction'. In *The Routledge Companion to Race and Ethnicity*, edited by Stephen M Caliendo and Charlton D. McIlwain, 1–5. London: Routledge.

Caliendo, Stephen M., and Charlton D. McIlwain, eds. 2021a. *The Routledge Companion to Race and Ethnicity*. Second ed. London: Routledge.

Casper, Lynne M., and Suzanne M. Bianchi. 2002. *Continuity and Change in the American Family*. Thousand Oaks: Sage Publications.

Cavalcante, Andre. 2015. 'Anxious Displacements: The Representation of Gay Parenting on Modern Family and The New Normal and the Management of Cultural Anxiety'. *Television & New Media* 16 (5):454–471.

Clinton, Elizabeth. 1622. *The Countesse of Lincolnes Nurserie*. Oxford.
Collins, Patricia Hill. 2009. *Black Feminist Thought*. 2nd edition. New York: Routledge.
Collins, Patricia Hill, and Sirma Bilge. 2020. *Intersectionality*. 2nd edition. Cambridge: Polity Press.
Combe, Andrew. 1860. *The Management of Infancy*. 9th edition. Edinburgh: Maclachlan and Stewart.
Connell, R. W. 2000. *The Men and the Boys*. Cambridge: Polity Press.
Connell, R. W. 2005. *Masculinities*. Berkeley: University of California Press.
Connell, R. W., and James W. Messerschmidt. 2005. 'Hegemonic Masculinity: Rethinking the Concept'. *Gender & Society* 19 (6):829–859.
Courtney, Jennifer. 2009. 'Real Men Do Housework: Ethos and Masculinity in Contemporary Domestic Advice'. *Rhetoric Review* 28 (1):66–81.
Criado-Perez, Caroline. 2019. *Invisible Women: Exposing Data Bias in a World Designed for Men*. London: Chatto & Windus.
Cunningham, Hugh. 2005. *Children and Childhood in Western Society Since 1500*. London: Pearson Education.
Currid-Halkett, Elizabeth. 2018. *The Sum of Small Things: A Theory of the Aspirational Class*. Princeton: Princeton University Press.
Darity Jr., William, Fenaba R. Addo, and Imari Z. Smith. 2021. 'A Subaltern Middle Class: The Case of the Missing 'Black Bourgeoisie' in America'. *Contemporary Economic Policy* 39 (3):494–502.
Davis, Angela. 2012. *Modern Motherhood: Women and Family in England 1945–2000*. Manchester: Manchester University Press.
De Benedictis, Sara. 2012. "Feral' Parents: Austerity Parenting Under Neoliberalism'. *Studies in the Maternal* 4 (2):1–21.
Devine, Fiona. 2005. 'MIddle-Class Identities in the United States'. In *Rethinking Class: Culture, Identities & Lifestyles*, edited by Fiona Devine, Mike Savage, John Scott and Rosemary Crompton, 140–162. Basingstoke: Palgrave Macmillan.
Doane, Janice, and Devon Hodges. 1993. *From Klein to Kristeva: Psychoanalytic Feminism and the Search for the 'Good Enough' Mother*. Ann Arbor: University of Michigan Press.
Dod, John, and Robert Cleaver. 1605. *A Plaine and Familiar Exposition of the Ten Commaundments*. London: Humfrey Lownes.
Dolby, Sandra K. 2005. *Self-Help Books: Why Americans Keep Reading Them*. Baltimore: University of Illinois Press.
Doucet, Andrea. 2016. 'Foreword'. In *Pops in Pop Culture: Fatherhood, Masculinity, and the New Man*, edited by Elizabeth Podnieks, ix–xii. Basingstoke: Palgrave Macmillan.
Doucet, Andrea. 2018. *Do Men Mother?* 2nd edition. Toronto: University of Toronto Press.
Douglas, Susan, and Meredith Michaels. 2005. *The Mommy Myth: The Idealization of Motherhood and How It Has Undermined All Women*. New York: Free Press.
Dow, Bonnie J. 2006. 'The Traffic in Men and the Fatal Attraction of Postfeminist Masculinity'. *Women's Studies in Communication* 29 (1):113–131.
Dowd, Nancy E. 2000. *Redefining Fatherhood*. New York: New York University Press.
Eccles, Audrey. 1982. *Obstetrics and Gynaecology in tudor and Stuart England*. London: Croom Helm.
Ehrenreich, Barbara, and Deirdre English. 2005. *For Her Own Good: Two Centuries of the Experts' Advice to Women*. Westminster: Knopf Publishing Group.
Ehrstein, Yvonne, Rosalind Gill, and Jo Littler. 2020. 'The Affective Life of Neoliberalism: Contructing (Un)reasonableness on Mumsnet'. In *Neoliberalism in Context: Governance,*

Subjectivity and Knowledge, edited by Simon Dawes and Marc Lenormand, 195–213. Palgrave Macmillan.
Ekman, Kajsa Ekis. 2021. *Om könets existens - tankar om den nya synen på kön*. Stockholm: Bokförlaget Polaris.
Elliott, Sinikka, Rachel Powell, and Joslyn Brenton. 2015. 'Being a Good Mom: Low-Income, Black Single Mothers Negotiate Intensive Mothering'. *Journal of Family Issues* 36 (3):351–370.
Erasmus of Rotterdam. 1965. *The Colloquies of Erasmus* 1526. Translated by Craig R. Thomspon. Chicago: The University of Chicago Press.
Faircloth, Charlotte, Diane M. Hoffman, and Linda L. Layne. 2013. 'Introduction'. In *Parenting in Global Perspective: Negotiating Ideologies of Kinship, Self and Politics*, edited by Charlotte Faircloth, Diane M. Hoffman and Linda L. Layne, 1–17. London: Routledge.
Farrell, Warren, and John Gray. 2018. *The Boy Crisis: Why Our Boys Are Struggling and What We Can Do About It*. Dallas: BenBella Books.
Fausto-Sterling, Anne. 2000. *Sexing the Body: Gender Politics and the Construction of Sexuality*. New York: Basic Books.
Fildes, Valerie. 1986. *Breasts, Bottles and Babies: a History of Infant Feeding*. Edinburgh: Edinburgh University Press.
Fine, Cordelia. 2010. *Delusions of Gender: How Our Minds, Society, and Neurosexism Create Difference*. New York: W. W. Norton & Company.
Fine, Cordelia. 2017. *Testosterone Rex : Myths of Sex, Science, and Society*. New York: W. W. Norton & Company.
Fleming, Linda M., and David J. Tobin. 2005. 'Popular Child-Rearing Books: Where Is Daddy?'. *Psychology of Men and Masculinity* 6 (1):18–24.
Furedi, Frank. 2008. *Paranoid Parenting: Why Ignoring the Experts May be Best for Your Child*. 3rd edition. London: Continuum.
Furstenberg, Frank. 1988. 'Good Dads - Bad Dads: Two Faces of Fatherhood'. In *The Changing American Family and Public Policy*, edited by Andrew J. Cherlin, 193–218. Washington D.C.: The Urban Institute Press.
Gavanas, Anna. 2004. *Fatherhood Politics in the United States: Masculinity, Sexuality, Race and Marriage*. Chicago: University of Illinois.
Gilbert, James. 2005. *Men in the Middle: Searching for Masculinity in the 1950s*. Chicago: The University of Chicago Press.
Gillis, John R. 2000. 'Marginalization of Fatherhood in Western Countries'. *Childhood* 7:225–238.
Golombok, Susan. 2015. *Modern Families: Parents and Children in New Family Forms*. Cambridge: Cambridge University Press.
Gottzén, Lucas. 2018. 'Is Masculinity Studies Really the 'Odd Man Out'?'. *NORMA* 13 (2):81–85.
Griswold, Robert L. 1993. *Fatherhood in America: A History*. New York: BasicBooks.
Gurian, Michael. 2006. *The Wonder of Boys: What Parents, Mentors, and Educators Can Do to Shape Boys into Exceptional Men*. London: Penguin Books.
Gurian, Michael. 2022. 'Gurian Institute'. accessed 16 Feb. https://gurianinstitute.com/.
Hamad, Hannah. 2014. *Postfeminism and Paternity in Contemporary U.S. Film: Framing Fatherhood*. New York: Routledge.
Hamamoto, Darrell Y. 1989. *Nervous Laughter: Television Situation Comedy and Liberal Democratic Ideology*. New York: Praeger.
Hancock, Ange-Marie. 2004. *The Politics of Disgust: The Public Identity of the Welfare Queen*. New York: New York University Press.

Haraway, Donna J. 1997. *Modest_Witness@Second_Millennium. FemaleMan©_Meets_ OncoMouse^TM*. New York: Routledge.
Hardyment, Christina. 2007. *Dream Babies: Childcare Advice from John Locke to Gina Ford*. London: Frances Lincoln Ltd.
Hays, Sharon. 1996. *The Cultural Contradictions of Motherhood*. New York: Yale University Press.
Haywood, Chris, and Mártín Mac an Ghaill. 2003. *Men and Masculinities*. Buckingham: Open University Press.
Hemez, Paul, and Chanell Washington. 2021. 'Number of Children Living With Only Their Mother Has Double in Last 50 Years'. Census Bureaur, accessed 16 Feb. https://www.census.gov/library/stories/2021/04/number-of-children-living-only-with-their-mothers-has-doubled-in-past-50-years.html#:~:text=With%20Mother%20Only-,Children%20living%20with%20a%20mother%20only%20is%20the%20second%20most,million%20(21%25)%20in%202020.
Hoffman, Diane M. 2009. 'How (Not) to Feel: Culture and the Politics of Emotion in the American Parenting Advice Literature'. *Discourse: Studies in the Cultural Politics of Education* 30 (1):15–31.
Humphreys, Kristi Rowan. 2016. 'Ads and Dads: TV Commercials and Contemporary Attitudes Toward Fatherhood'. In *Pops in Pop Culture: Fatherhood, Masculinity, and the New Man*, edited by Elizabeth Podnieks, 107–124. Basingstoke: Palgrave Macmillan.
Hunter, Sarah C., and Damien W. Riggs. 2015. 'Hegemonic Masculinities and Heteronormativities in Contemporary Books on Fathering and Raising Boys'. *Boyhood Studies* 8 (1):110–129.
Hunter, Sarah C., Damien W. Riggs, and Martha Augoustinos. 2017. 'Hegemonic Masculinity Versus a Caring Masculinity: Implications for Understanding Primary Caregiving Fathers'. *Social and Personality Pscyhology Compass* 11 (3):1–9.
Hunter, Sarah C., Damien W. Riggs, and Martha Augoustinos. 2020. 'Constructions of Primary Caregiving Fathers in Popular Parenting Texts'. *Men and Masculinities* 23 (1):150–169.
Hyde, Janet Shibley. 2005. 'The Gender Similarities Hypothesis'. *American Psychologist* 60 (6):581–592.
James, Shawn. 2013. 'Ways Single Mothers Destroy Their Sons'. *Shawn James, Black Freelance Writer*, 16 Feb 2022.
Jenkins, Candice M. 2007. *Private Lives, Proper Relations: Regulating Black Intimacy*. Minneapolis: University of Minnesota Press.
Jensen, Robert. 2021. 'Whiteness'. In *The Routledge Companion to Race and Ethnicity*, edited by Stephen M Caliendo and Charlton D. McIlwain, 25–32. London: Routledge.
Joel, Daphna, Zohar Berman, Ido Tavor, Nadav Wexler, Olga Gaber, Yaniv Stein, Nisan Shefi, Jared Pool, Sebastian Urchs, Daniel S. Margulies, Franziskus Liem, Jürgen Hänggi, Jäncke Lutz, and Yaniv Assaf. 2015. 'Sex beyond the Genitalia: The Human Brain Mosaic'. *Proceedings of the National Academy of Sciences of the United States of America* 112 (50):15468–15473.
Johansen, Shawn. 2001. *Family Men: Middle-Class Fatherhood in Early Industrializing America*. New York: Routledge.
Jones, Janelle, and John Schmitt. 2014. 'A College Degree is No Guarantee'. Center for Economic and Policy Research. https://www.cepr.net/documents/black-coll-grads-2014-05.pdf.
Kimmel, Michael. 2012. *Manhood in America: a Cultural History*. 3rd edition. Oxford: Oxford Universit Press.

Kimmel, Michael. 2013. *Angry White Men: American Masculinity at the End of an Era*. New York: Nation Books.
King, Joyce Elaine, and Carolyn Ann Mitchell. 1995. *Black Mothers to Sons: Juxtaposing African American Literature with Social Practice*. New York: Peter Lang.
Kingston, Paul W. 2000. *The Classless Society*. Stanford: Stanford University Press.
Krafchick, Jennifer L., Toni Schindler Zimmerman, Shelley A. Haddock, and James H. Banning. 2005. 'Best-Selling Books Advising Parents about Gender: A Feminist Analysis'. *Family Relations* 54:84–100.
Labor, Statistics Bureau of. 2016. 'A Profile of the Working Poor, 2014'. U.S. Bureau of Labor Statistcis, accessed 3 March. https://www.bls.gov/opub/reports/working-poor/2014/home.htm.
Lareau, Anette. 2000. 'My Wife Can Tell Me Who I Know: Methodological and Conceptual Problems in Studying Fathers'. *Qualitative Sociology* 23 (4):407–433.
Lareau, Anette. 2008. 'Watching, Waiting, and Deciding When to Intervene: Race, Class, and the Transmission of Advantage'. In *The Way Class Works: Readings on School, Family, and the Economy*, edited by Lois Weis, 117–133. New York: Routledge.
Lareau, Anette. 2011. *Unequal Childhoods: Class, Race, and Family Life*. 2nd edition. Berkeley: University of California Press.
LaRossa, Ralph. 1997. *The Modernization of Fatherhood: A Social and Political History*. Chicago: Chicago University Press.
Lee, Ellie, Jennie Bristow, Charlotte Faircloth, and Jan Macvarish, eds. 2014. *Parenting Culture Studies*. Basingstoke: Palgrave Macmillan.
Lee, John. 2015. *Breaking the Mother-Son Dynamic: Resetting the Patterns of a Man's Life and Loves*. Deerfield Beach, FL: Health Communiations Inc.
Leverenz, David. 2003. *Paternalism Incorporated: Fables of American Fatherhood, 1865–1940*. Ithaca: Cornell University Press.
Littlefield, Marci Bounds. 2008. 'The Media as a System of Racialization: Exploring Images of African American Women and the New Racism'. *American Behavioral Science* 51 (5):675–685.
Love, Patricia. 1990. *The Emotional Incest Syndrome: What to Do When a Parent's Love Rules Your Life*. New York: Bantam Books.
Macvarish, Jan. 2016. *Neuroparenting: The Expert Invasion of Family Life*. Basingstoke: Palgrave Macmillan.
Macvarish, Jan, Ellie Lee, and Pam Lowe. 2014. 'The 'First three Years' Movement and the Infant Brain: A Review of Critiques'. *Sociology Compass* 8 (6):792–804.
Marquis, Nicolas. 2019. 'Taking One's Responsibilities While Facing Adversity: A Balanced Analysis of Self-Help Books Reading'. *Sociological Research Online* 24 (2):137–153.
Marsh, Kris, William A. Darity Jr., Philip N. Cohen, Lynne M. Casper, and Danielle Salters. 2007. 'The Emerging Black Middle Class: Single and Living Alone'. *Social Forces* 86 (2):753–762.
Marsiglio, William, and Joseph H Pleck. 2005. 'Fatherhood and Masculinities'. In *Handbook of Studies on Men and Masculinities*, edited by Michael S. Kimmel, Jeff Hearn and Raewyn Connell, 249–269. Thousand Oaks, CA: SAGE Publications.
McGee, Micki. 2005. *Self-Help Inc.: Makeover Culture in American Life*. Oxford: Oxford University Press.
McIntosh, Dawn Marie D. 2018. 'From White Ladies to White Trash Mamas: (Re) Locating the Performances of White Femininity'. In *Interrogating the Communicative*

Power of Whiteness, edited by Dawn Marie D. McIntosh, Dreama G. Moon and Thomas K. Nakayama, 94–116. New York: Routledge.

Messner, Michael A. 2016. 'On Patriarchs and Losers: Rethinking Men's Interests'. In *Exploring Masculinities: Identity, Inequality, Continuity, and Change*, edited by C. J. Pascoe and Tristan Bridges, 198–206. Oxford: Oxford University Press.

Mills, Martin. 2003. 'Shaping the Boys' Agenda: the Backlash Blockbusters'. *International Journal of Inclusive Education* 7 (1):57–73.

Molasses. 2013. 'Entertaining'. Amazon.com, accessed 3 March. https://www.amazon.com/gp/customer-reviews/R4TPXJESTSZLH/ref=cm_cr_getr_d_rvw_ttl?ie=UTF8&ASIN=B007KLYUEO.

Moya, Paula M. L., and Hazel Rose Markus. 2010. 'Doing Race: An Introduction'. In *Doing Race: 21 Essays for the 21st Century*, edited by Hazel Rose Markus and Paula M. L. Moya, 1–102. New York: W. W. Norton.

Moynihan, Daniel Patrick. 1967. 'The Negro Family: The Case for National Action'. In *The Moynihan Report and the Politics of Controversy*, edited by Lee Rainwater and William L. Yancey, 41–124. Cambridge, MA: The M.I.T. Press.

Nakamura, Janice. 2021. 'English Parenting for Japanese Parents: A Critical Review of Advice in Self-Help Books for Raising Bilingual Children in Japan'. *English Today*:1–6.

Pascoe, C. J., and Tristan Bridges. 2016a. 'Introduction - Exploring Masculinities: History, Reproduction, Hegemony, and Dislocation'. In *Exploring Masculinities: Identity, Inequality, Continuity, and Change*, edited by C. J. Pascoe and Tristan Bridges, 1–34. Oxford: Oxford University Press.

Pascoe, C. J., and Tristan Bridges. 2016b. 'Historizing Masculinities: An Introduction'. In *Exploring Masculinities: Identity, Inequality, Continuity, and Change*, edited by C. J. Pascoe and Tristan Bridges, 37–49. Oxford: Oxford University Press.

Pehlke, Timothy Allen, Charles B. Hennon, M. Elise Radina, and Katherine A. Kuvalanka. 2009. 'Does Father Still Know Best? An Inductive Thematic Analysis of Popular TV Sitcoms'. *Fathering: A Journal of Theory, Research, and Practice about Men as Fathers* 7 (2):114–139.

Plant, Rebecca Jo. 2010. *Mom: The Transformation of Motherhood in Modern America*. Chicago: The University of Chicago Press.

Podnieks, Elizabeth. 2016. 'Introduction: Pops in Pop Context'. In *Pops in Pop Culture: Fatherhood, Masculinity, and the New Man*, edited by Elizabeth Podnieks, 1–27. Basingstoke: Palgrave Macmillan.

Pollack, William. 1998. *Real Boys: Rescuing Our Sons from the Myths of Boyhood*. New York: Random House.

Popenoe, David. 1999. *Life without Father : Compelling New Evidence that Fatherhood and Marriage are Indispensable for the Good of Children and Society*. London: Harvard University Press.

Pugh, Tison. 2018. 'Conservative Narratology, Queer Politics, and the Humor of Gay Stereotypes in Modern Family'. In *The Queer Fantasies of the American Family Sitcom*, 161–189. New Brunswick: Rutgers University Press.

Raeburn, Paul. 2014. *Do Fathers Matter? What Science Is Telling Us About the Parent We've Overlooked*. New York: Scientific American / Farrar, Straus and Giroux.

Rothman, Barbara Katz. 2009. 'Mothering Alone: Rethinking Single Motherhood in America'. *Woman's Studies Quarterly* 37 (3 & 4):323–328.

Sandretto, Susan, and Karen Nairn. 2019. 'Do Parenting Advice Books Help or Harm? Critiquing 'Common-Sense' Advice for Mothers Raising Boys'. *Gender and Education* 31 (3):327–343.

Sato, Hiroaki, Isamu Sando, and Haruo Takahashi. 1991. 'Sexual Dimporphism and Development of the Human Cochlea: computer 3-D Measurement'. *Acta Oto-Laryngologica* 111 (6):1037–1040.

Sax, Leonard. 2016. *Boys Adrift: The Five Factors Driving the Growing Epidemic of Unmotivated Boys and Underachieving Young Men*. New York: Basic Books.

Schmitz, Rachel M. 2016. 'Constructing Men as Fathers: A Content Analysis of Formulations of Fatherhood in Parenting Magazines'. *Journal of Men's Studies* 24 (1):3–23.

Schrock, Douglas, and Michael Schwalbe. 2009. 'Men, Masculinity, and Manhood Acts'. *Annual Review of Sociology* 35:277–295.

Sharp, Jane. 1671. *The Midwives Book*. London: Simon Miller.

Skeggs, Beverley. 1997. *Formations of Class and Gender: Becoming Respectable*. London: SAGE.

Skeggs, Beverley. 2004. *Class, Self, Culture*. London: Routledge.

Skelton, Christine. 2001. *Schooling the Boys: Masculinities and Primary Education*. Buckingham: Open University Press.

Skelton, Christine. 2002. 'The 'Feminisation of Schooling' or "Re-masculinising' Primary Education'. *International Studies in Sociology of Education* 12 (1):77–96.

Skelton, Christine, and Becky Francis. 2009. *Feminism and "The Schooling Scandal"*. London: Routledge.

Sommers, Christina Hoff. 2013. *The War Against Boys: How Misguided Policies Are Harming Our Young Men*. London: Simon & Schuster.

Spencer, Stephen. 2014. *Race and Ethnicity: Culture, Identity and Representation*. London: Routledge.

Statista. 2021. 'Number of Children Living with a Single Mother or a Single Father in the U.S. from 1970 to 2020', accessed 28 Feb. https://www.statista.com/statistics/252847/number-of-children-living-with-a-single-mother-or-single-father/.

Stearns, Peter N. 2003. *Anxious Parents: A History of Modern Childrearing in America*. New York: New York University.

Strecker, Edward. 1947. *Their Mothers' Sons: The Psychiatrist Exmaines an American Problem*. Philadelphia. 201.

Sunderland, Jane. 2006. '"Parenting" or "Mothering"? The Case of Modern Childcare Magazines'. *Discourse & Society* 17 (4):503–527.

Tarrant, Anna, Gareth Terry, Michael R. M. Ward, Sandy Ruxton, Martin Robb, and Brigid Featherstone. 2015. 'Are Male Role Models Really the Solution? Interrogating the 'War on Boys' Through the Lens of 'Male Role Model' Discourse'. *Boyhood Studies* 8 (1):60–83.

Thorne, Barrie. 1994. *Gender Play: Girls and Boys in School*. New Brunswick: Rutgers University Press.

Titus, Jordan J. 2004. 'Boy Trouble: Rhetorical Framing of Boys' Underachievement'. *Discourse: Studies in the Cultural Politics of Education* 25 (2):145–169.

Tomaskovic-Devey, Donald, Melvin Thomas, and Kecia Johnson. 2005. 'Race and the Accumulation of Human Capital across the Career: A Theoretical Model and Fixed-Effects Application'. *American Journal of Sociology* 111 (1):58–89. doi: 10.1086/431779.

Van der Graaff, Jolien, Susan Branje, Minet De Wied, Skyler Hawk, Pol Van Lier, and Wim Meeus. 2014. 'Perspective Taking and Emphatic Concern in Adolescence: Gender Differences in Developmental Changes'. *Developmental Psychology* 50 (3):881–888.

Vavrus, Mary Douglas. 2002. 'Domesticating Patriarchy: Hegemonic Masculinity and Television's 'Mr. Mom''. *Critical Studies in Media Communication* 19 (3):352–375.

Wahlström Henriksson, Helena, and Disa Bergnehr. 2021. 'Hardworking Women: Representations of Lone Mothers in Swedish Daily Press'. *Feminist Media Studies* 21 (1):132–146.

Waling, Andrea. 2019. 'Rethinking Masculinity Studies: Feminism, Masculinity, and Poststructural Accounts of Agency and Emotional Reflexivity'. *Journal of Men's Studies* 27 (1):89–107.

Wall, Glenda, and Stephanie Arnold. 2007. 'How Involved is Involved Fathering? An Exploration of the Contemporary Culture of Fatherhood'. *Gender & Society* 21 (4):508–527.

Walton, F. Carl, and Stephen M. Caliendo. 2021. 'Origins of the Concept of Race'. In *The Routledge Companion to Race and Ethnicity*, edited by Stephen M. Caliendo and Charlton D. McIlwain, 10–17. London: Routledge.

Weis, Lois. 2008. 'Toward a Re-thinking of Class as Nested in Race and Gender: Tracking the White Working Class in the Final Quarter of the Twentieth Century'. In *The Way Class Works: Readings on School, Family, and the Economy*, edited by Lois Weis, 291–304. New York: Routledge.

Weiss, Nancy Pottishman. 1978. 'The Mother-Child Dyad Revisited: Perceptions of Mothers and Children in Twentieth Century Child-Rearing Manuals'. *Journal of Social Issues* 34 (2):29–45.

Williams, Joan C. 2020. *White Working Class: Overcoming Class Cluelessness in America*. Boston: Harvard Business Reivew Press.

Wylie, Philip. 1942. *Generation of Vipers*. New York.

INDEX

7 Principles for Raising Black Sons: A Practical Hand-Guide for Today's Single Black Mothers (Estelle) 40

Accomando, Christina 2
Adair, Vivyan 44
Adams, John 58
Adams, Michele 21, 27, 73
African American(s) 41, 59; authors 48–52, 54, 55, 57, 60, 61, 63, 64; bourgeoisie 43; children 50; family structures 61; fathers 61; female bodies 46; men 51; single mothers 3, 45–47, 56, 60–64; students 51–52; women 45–47, 60, 61, 63
Allen, Mardi 12, 25, 27, 28, 30–33, 35, 50, 55, 62, 63, 69, 71
Amazon 1, 10, 77, 78
American families 3; structures 4–5, 11, 33, 66, 78; tradition and change 3–5
Anderson, Antonio 26
Anderson, Kristin J. 2, 75
anti-boy culture 2
Apple, Rima 5
artificial reproductive technologies (ARTs) 3, 4, 12, 78
ARTs, *see* artificial reproductive technologies
aspirational class 43
Atlantic Publishing Group 10
attitude 3, 19, 49; gendered cultural 38; neoliberal 7; societal 65
authoritarian father 66
autism 6

Barnett, Rosalind 18, 73
Barth, Fredrik 22
Bauman, Zygmunt 58
Bay and Her Boys (Buchanan) 78
Beasley, Chris 21
Berggren, Kalle 21

Bianchi, Suzanne 3
Biddulph, Steve 10, 25, 26
Bilge, Sirma 38
biological determinism 23
biological differences 15–17, 24
Black Feminist Thought (Collins) 60
Blakes, R. C. 74
Blankenhorn, David 4, 68
Bly, Robert 32
Bolds, Denise 35, 52, 54, 57, 60, 61
borderwork and gender 22–27; boys and girls 26–27; mothers and fathers 27–30; mothers and sons 23–25
Bourne, Mervin, Jr. 31, 41, 49, 54, 55
Bowlby, John 6
Boy Crisis, The (Farrell and Gray) 8
Boyd-Franklin, Nancy 40
boys: behaviour around police officers 54; fatherless 28–30; in school environment 26–27
Boys Adrift: The Five Factors Driving the Growing Epidemic of Unmotivated Boys and Underachieving Men (Sax) 8
brain 18; boy's 25, 26; male *vs.* female 17, 24–26; structure 17
Bridges, Tristan 19, 20
Bromfield, Richard 12, 24, 25, 27, 34, 35, 50, 55, 59, 60, 62, 63
Bryant, Christopher K. 48, 61, 71
Buchanan, Bay 40, 43, 50, 53–55, 57, 58, 60, 62, 71, 78
Bull, Thomas 5
Bundy, Ted 32
Butler, Judith 16

Cadogan, William 5, 9
Caliendo, Stephen M. 38–40
Casper, Lynne 3
Center for Economic and Policy Research 51

Chavasse, Pye Henry 5
childcare 19; government policy on 57; medicalization of 5
child/children: born out of wedlock 4; brain development 6, 7; mental and emotional health 6; mortality 5; support payments 71; as vulnerability 5–6
childrearing 2, 3, 5–7, 19, 43, 56, 69
Chisholm, Dana 51, 55, 58, 62, 71, 72
civil rights movement 45, 66
class 3, 37, 41–44, 48–49
Class, Self, Culture (Skeggs) 42
Clinton, Elizabeth 9
Collins, Patricia Hill 13, 38, 41, 45, 46, 60
Coltrane, Scott 21, 27
Combe, Andrew 5, 9
concerted cultivation 44, 49, 57
Connell, Raewyn 20, 21
conservative Christianity 22
contemporary cultural norms 2
contemporary society 11
corpus callosum 17, 24
Countess of Lincoln 9
Courtney, Jennifer 12, 75
CreateSpace 10
Cultural Contradictions of Motherhood, The (Hays) 42, 49
culture: African American 40, 41; anti-studying 50; difference 23; traditions 42
Currid-Halkett, Elizabeth 43, 50

dad-deprivation 8, 28
Darity, William 43
De Benedictis, Sara 1, 7
Delusions of Gender (Fine) 17
Dennis, John P. 11, 12, 27, 32, 34, 48, 61, 65, 69–72, 75
Devine, Fiona 41
Dickerson, James 12, 25, 27, 28, 30–33, 35, 48, 50, 55, 62, 63, 69, 71
Do Men Mother? (Doucet) 22
Doing Race (Markus and Moya) 40
Dolby, Sandra 2, 9–11, 77
Doucet, Andrea 11, 22, 32
Dowd, Nancy E. 31, 61, 68, 70

education 43, 49–52
Edwards, Brian 74
ego development 31
Elium, Don 30, 32
Elium, Jeanne 30, 32
Elliott, Sinikka 56, 58

emotional development 11
emotional incest syndrome 29
endocrinology 24
Engber, Andrea 73
Erasmus of Rotterdam 9
Erhardt, Anke 15
Erwin, Cheryl 12, 24, 25, 27, 34, 35, 50, 55, 60, 62, 63
Essay upon Nursing and the Management of Children from their Birth to Three Years of Age, An (Cadogan) 5
Estelle, Khaz 49, 55
ethnicity 38, 39, 41
Exploring Masculinities (Pascoe and Bridges) 19

Faircloth, Charlotte 6
Faludi, Susan 67
family: concept of 3–4; pathology 45; traditional 33
Farrell, William 8, 28, 68
'father absence' ('fatherlessness') 4, 28
Father-Daughter Talk, The (Blakes) 74
fatherhood 4, 65, 66–68, 70
fathering 69, 70, 72
Fatherless America (Blankenhorn) 4
fathers: absent/staying away 70–71; counternarratives 71–73; *vs.* mothers 69–70; raising daughters 73–76; representations in media and popular culture 66–68
Fausto-Sterling, Anne 16, 17, 19
feminism/femininity/feminization 11, 26, 37, 50
feminist movement 7, 26, 66
financial disparities 38
Fine, Cordelia 17–19
Formations of Class and Gender (Skeggs) 42
Franklin, A. J. 40, 48
From Good Ma to Welfare Queen (Adair) 44
Furedi, Frank 6, 23, 56
Furstenberg, Frank 70
Future of Marriage, The (Blankenhorn) 68

gender 2, 3; boundaries 22–23; confusion 35; as dichotomy 22; fluidity 16, 22; identity 35; issues 35; sex and 15–22
Generation of Vipers (Wylie) 66
George, Jessica 2
Gilbert, James 67
Golombok, Susan 3
Gray, John 8, 28, 68
Gross, Gretchen 75

Guide to Heaven (Hardy) 9
Gurian, Michael 2, 7, 8
Gurian Institute 8

Hall, Philip 23
Hamad, Hannah 67
Hancock, Ange-Marie 44, 46
Haraway, Donna 17
Hardy, Samuel 9
Hays, Sharon 37, 42, 43, 49–51, 53
hegemonic masculinity 19, 21, 31, 32
heteronormativity 33–36; compulsory heterosexuality 34–36; threat of sexuality 33–34; view of family 33
heterosexuality 4, 5, 34–36
Hispanics 52
Hoffman, Diane M. 6
homophobia 35
homosexuality 34, 35
Howland, MaryAnne 12, 33, 51, 71, 72, 74, 75
human conduct 17, 18
Humphreys, Kristie Rowan 20
Hunter, Sarah C. 2, 65, 69
hybrid masculinity 19, 20
Hyde, Janet Shibley 18, 19

identity 22; Black 41; construction 16; gender 21, 35; masculine 20; middle-class 41, 42
intensive mothering 43, 56, 57
intersectional approach 37, 38, 58
Intersectionality (Collins and Bilge) 38
intersex people 16, 22
Iron Hans (Bly) 32

James, Shawn 1
Jenkins, Candice 45, 64
Johnson, Rick 29, 31
Jones, LaVeda M. 9, 55
Joyce, Donna 10, 31, 71

Kennedy, Neil 55
King, Darrell W. 52
Kingston, Paul W. 41
Klumpp, Mike 75
Klungness, Leah 73
Krause, Tina 55

Lareau, Anette 40, 42, 44, 49, 50, 56, 68
LaRossa, Ralph 66
Layne, Linda L. 6
legal matters 53–54

Leman, Kevin 74
lesbian partnerships 3, 5, 33
Lewis, Franklin Donny D. 58
Livingston, Patricia 75

Macvarish, Jan 6, 8, 19, 28
male privilege and power 30
male role models 12, 19, 30, 32–35, 59, 73, 74
Man & Woman, Boy & Girl (Money and Erhardt) 15
manhood 31
Markus, Hazel Rose 40, 41
Marquis, Nicolas 77
marriages 4, 11
Marsh, Kris 42
Marsiglio, William 4, 70, 72
masculinity 15, 19–22, 27, 37, 67, 69, 72; teaching 30–33
maternal education movement 2
maternal gatekeeping 68, 71
maternal inadequacy 6
maternal sexuality 59–61
matriarchy 45
matrifocality 45
McGee, Micki 1, 9
McIlwain, Charlton 38, 39
McIntosh, Dawn Marie 46, 47
Meeker, Meg 9, 10, 12, 23, 25, 28, 31, 55, 62, 72–74, 77
men bodies 20
men raised by women (MRW) 32
metrosexuality 19, 20, 32
middle class 44; Black 42, 43; concept of 43; parents 50; White 40, 42, 43, 47, 49; White authors 47, 49–51, 53, 55; women 67
Midwives Book, The (Sharp) 5
Mills, Martin 7
Moffitt, Betina 52
Momism 66
Money, John 15
Moore, Derrick 61
moral development 12
morality 49
mother-enmeshed men 29
motherhood: practices 43; White 47
mother(s): Black 50, 51; dating 60, 61; expectations placed on 56–59; middle-class 49, 51; not able to be father 29–30; pathogenic 28–29; *see also* single mother(s)
Moya, Paula M. L. 40, 41

Moynihan, Daniel Patrick 45
MRI analysis 18
MRW, *see* men raised by women
'My Wife Can Tell Me Who I Know'
    (Lareau) 68

Nairn, Karen 3
Nease, Jessica 2
*Negro Family: The Cause for National Action,
    The* (1965) 45
neoliberalism 22
neuroparenting 6, 8, 24, 49
new dad 19, 20
'new families' 3
Nilsen, Ann 58
Norwood, Lisa 30

Palmer, Shondreka 60, 63, 64
Panettieri, Gina 23, 25–27, 33–36, 40, 50,
    54, 57, 72, 73
paranoid parenting 23, 56
Paranoid Parenting (Furedi) 6
parental anxiety 5, 6
parental responsibilities 11
parenting 2, 3, 6–7, 11, 15, 17, 19, 67–69
Parenting in Global Perspective (Faircloth,
    Hoffman and Layne) 6
Pascoe, C. J. 19, 20
Passley, Josef A. 10
Pearson, Jenieka L. 52, 58, 61, 62, 71
personal finances 52–53
Phillips, Patrick 25, 40, 52
physical and emotional toughness 30
Pleck, Joseph 4, 70, 72
political correctness 11, 25
*Politics of Disgust: The Public Identity of the
    Welfare Queen, The* (Hancock) 44
Pollack, William 2
Popenoe, David 4, 68
postfeminist fatherhood 67
*Private Lives, Proper Relations: Regulating
    Black Intimacy* (Jenkins) 45

race 3, 37–41; difference 56; neutrality 39
*Race and Ethnicity: Culture, Identity and
    Representation* (Spencer) 39
racism 40, 59
Raeburn, Paul 68
'*Raising a Prince without a King*' (Jones) 9
*Raising Boys: Why Boys Are Different - and
    How to Help Them Become Happy and
    Well-Balanced Men* (Biddulph) 10

Random House 10
Real Boys (Pollack) 2
Redefining Fatherhood (Dowd) 68
religion 55–56
Riggs, Damien W. 2
Rivers, Caryl 18, 73
Rothman, Barbara Katz 78
*Routledge Companion to Race and Ethnicity,
    The* (Caliendo and McIlwain) 38
Ruddick, Sarah 11

Saddam Hussein 32
*Same Difference: How Gender Myths Are
    Hurting Our Relationships, Our Children,
    and Our Jobs* (Barnett and Rivers) 18
same-sex desire: *see* homosexuality
Sandretto, Susan 3
Sax, Leonard 8, 26
Schrock, Douglas 31
Schwalbe, Michael 31
self-sacrifice 56
sex: aggression 46; assaults 46; differences
    17–20; orientation 35; production 46
sex and gender 15–22; brain and sex
    differences 16–19; masculinity studies
    19–22
Sexing the Body (Fausto-Sterling) 16
sexuality 33–34
Sharp, Jane 9
Simon & Schuster 10
*Single Dad's Survival Guide: How to Succeed as
    a One-Man Parenting Team, The* (Klumpp)
    75
single mother(s) 1, 77; Black 58; chidren
    live in 4; class, race and stereotypes
    44–47; households 5; ways of being 12
Single Mother's Guide to Raising Black Boys
    (Lewis) 40
Skeggs, Beverley 42, 44
Skelton, Christine 26
slavery 45, 58
Small, William C. 10, 28, 31, 65, 70
social injustice 23
social problems 7, 38
sociocultural differences 18
Sommers, Christina Hoff 8
Spencer, Stephen 39
Starker, Steven 9, 12
Stearns, Peter 5
stereotypes 2, 17, 24, 25, 45–47, 63, 64, 77
strategic essentialism 21
Strecker, Edward 66

Strong Mothers, Strong Sons: Lessons Mothers Need to Raise Extraordinary Men (Meeker) 9, 77–78
Swanson, Monica 34, 57, 62

Tardy, Cederick 51
Tarrant, Anna 32
technoscientific body 17
testosterone 17, 18, 24
Testosterone Rex (Fine) 18
Their Mother's Sons (Strecker) 66
Thorne, Barrie 22
Tomaskovic-Devey, Donald 52
toxic parents 19
transgender issues 16
Tyler, Jamie 53, 60

Unequal Childhoods (Lareau) 42, 49
Unfriendly World Children 32
United States 1, 2, 5, 41, 44, 50; society 1, 15, 22, 41, 44, 55, 59; socio-economic upheavals in 66
US Census 4

Vavrus, Mary Douglas 20

Waling, Andrea 21
Walton, F. Carl 40
War Against Boys: How Misguided Policies Are Harming Our Young Men, The (Sommers) 8
Watkins, Deborah 40, 41, 43, 51–55, 59, 61, 63
'Ways Single Mothers Destroy Their Sons' (James) 1
Weis, Lois 41
Weiss, Nancy Pottisham 2
Western culture 56, 59
White: authors 39, 44, 47–49, 54, 55, 57, 60, 64; mothers 3, 56, 59; privilege 40, 54; working-class 55, 64
Williams, Joan C. 42, 44, 48, 50, 55
Winnicott, Donald 6, 56
Wonder of Boys: What Parents, Mentors, and Educators Can Do to Shape Boys into Exceptional Men, The (Gurian) 2, 7
working class 41–44; Black 49; British 41, 44; mothers 47, 49; White women 46, 49
World War II 44, 66
Wylie, Philip 66

www.ingramcontent.com/pod-product-compliance
Lightning Source LLC
Chambersburg PA
CBHW021146230426
43667CB00005B/270